The Things That Make Men Cry

The Things That Make Men Cry

∞

Gloria Morrow, Ph.D.

Foreword by Bishop Eddie L. Long

The Things That Make Men Cry

∞

Gloria Morrow, Ph.D.

Shining Glory Publications, Inc.

Upland, California

Published by Shining Glory Publications, Inc.
308 N. 2nd Avenue
Upland, California 91786
(909) 985-0072

All Scripture quotations unless otherwise noted are taken from the Holy Bible: New King James Version Copyright @1982 by Thomas Nelson, Inc. Used by permission. All rights reserves.

Publisher's Note
The information in this book is true and complete to the best of the author and publisher's knowledge. However, the names, and other pertinent details concerning individuals in this book have been changed. This book is intended only as an information reference and should not replace, countermand, or conflict with the advice given to readers by their professional marriage therapists, mental health providers, and/or physicians. It is sold with the understanding that the author and publisher are not engaged in rendering medical, mental health, psychological, or any other kind of personal or professional services in the book. The reader should consult her or his culturally competent marriage therapist, mental health professional, and/or physician before adopting any of the suggestions in this book or drawing inferences from it. The author and publisher disclaim all liability in connection with the specific personal use of any and all information provided in this book.

Morrow, Gloria, 1950-
    The Things that Make Men Cry/by Gloria Morrow. - 1st ed. p.cm.

Includes Selected Bibliography
Library of Congress Control Number: 2003115310
ISBN 0-9747168-3-9
Printed and bound in the United States of America

This book is dedicated to the men who have taught me the most about the inner workings and complexities surrounding manhood: my husband, Rev. Tommy Morrow, my son, Steven Wayne, and my father, Rev. Harold Phillips. It is because of your honesty, transparency, and love that I, a woman, could even dare to write such a book. I also dedicate this book to my Savior, Jesus Christ, who not only teaches me important lessons about men daily, but continues to teach me how to work in peace and harmony with them.

∞

TABLE OF CONTENT

∞

ACKNOWLEDGMENTS

I will be forever grateful to the following 14 men who allowed their voices to be heard in this project: Stan Alli, Leonard Aubrey, Rob Coachman, Berkeley Harris, Philip Jacobs, Daniel Miller, Rev. Harold Phillips, Pastor Tommy Morrow, Tommy Smalley, Tommy Steward, Vernon Ware, Donnie Washington, Steven Wayne, and Nate Wicks. without your voices, this project would have been incomplete. I am especially grateful to my friend and brother, Bishop Eddie L. Long, Senior Pastor of the New Birth Missionary Baptist Church, in Lithonia, Georgia for agreeing to write the Foreword for this book. I would also like to acknowledge the creative work of Damien Dunn, who designed the original cover for this book, Alexander Hickman who designed the current cover, and Siblatha Graphics for layout and design. May your lives be richly blessed in every endeavor you undertake to enrich the Kingdom of God.

The Things that Make Men Cry

∞

Gloria Morrow, Ph.D.

Foreword by Bishop Eddie L. Long

FOREWORD

Imagine with me that you are holding one of those heavy duty trash bags. You know the ones...they are advertised as being able to handle anything that you put in it. So you try it. You clean out the refrigerator and dump two weeks' worth of leftovers into the heavy duty bag.

You then go into your bedroom and clean out all of the newspapers, bottled water, and whatever else you can find. You aren't done yet. You take your foot and push all of the trash further down in the bag and then make your way to the garage. You throw a few of your child's broken toys and the old paint cans into the bag.

Finally, you end up in the front yard and you pile leaves, rocks, and grass into the heavy duty trash bag. Satisfied with your cleaning project you decide to lift the trash bag up and place it into the trash can for the sanitation company. However, you've run into a problem. As you pick it up, the heavy duty bag actually bursts at the bottom and all of the contents fall out. You realize that although it's advertised as a heavy duty trash bag, you've put way more in it than it was created to hold.

What does the above scenario have to do with **"The Things that Make Men Cry?"** Well, think about it. Isn't that what goes on with most men? Haven't we been 'advertised' as being able to handle it all?

Most of us have been raised, conditioned, taught and bullied into believing that we are 'heavy duty' men and that we can handle anything that comes at us. We have been conditioned to simply push our issues as far down as possible so that we can handle more of what life throws at us. But just like that heavy duty trash bag, at some point, when it's time for us to actually get up and move towards destiny, move into our promise or even move into a new season in our lives, we break.

Often the break is subtle...we stop speaking to our wives; we yell at our children; we hide behind our titles and our positions. However, the longer we sit in silence we are setting ourselves up for a more extreme break...and unfortunately when that happens so many of our loved ones may be devastatingly harmed as a result.

Don't get me wrong. I believe that God created men with a supernatural ability to handle the weight of life. I am still what the young people consider 'ole fashioned. I believe that women are a precious commodity (and they too hide a secret pain, but that's another story for another time) and while they have a strength that has often been overlooked and belittled, it is a different type of strength than that of a man. Neither is better...they are just different.

Men are warriors and therefore there are certain struggles, fights and issues that are unique to them. So again, I believe that men are called to handle certain issues, but there is one important fact that we often forget: we aren't called to handle them alone. We aren't called to suppress our emotions or to stomp around like King Kong, with an invincible mentality.

So what do we do? I believe that in the pages of this book, you will find a road map that will direct you to the Word of God and ultimately to a path of freedom. Dr. Morrow has successfully married the power of scripture with the study of mental health. By opening up the pages of **"The Things that Make Men Cry,"** you will be able to finally scream 'uncle'…you will finally be able to say enough is enough. Through her sensitive, transparent, yet no-nonsense style, Dr. Morrow uses her clinical training and Biblical understanding to expose the pain that so many of us try to cover up.

In addition, realizing that according to Revelations 12:11, "…we overcome by the word of our testimony…;" Dr. Morrow interviewed 14 men and she uses their testimonies to assist the reader in relating to the issues presented.

To the male reader: I challenge you to 'man-up'…but not in the traditional way we've understood that statement to mean. I challenge you to 'man-up' to the truth that you are not an island unto yourself. You have a wife, a daughter, a son, a mother, a nephew, a sister, a co-worker, a friend that needs you. But they don't need the empty 'you'. They need the 'you' that God created you to be. Allow God to use his daughter, Dr. Morrow to help you peel back years of hidden pain, hurt and disappointment so that you can be healed and whole.

To the female reader: **"The Things that Make Men Cry"** is not just for men. It is for you as well. Dr. Morrow's candid and direct style of teaching will help you to recognize what is behind the wall of the men in your life. Ask God to allow you to see through His eyes so that you can see the man beneath the anger...beneath the silence...beneath the aloofness. Allow God to create sensitivity in your heart that will lead to a renewed relationship with your loved ones. (Note: If you are in a dangerous situation, you should seek help to remove yourself safely and quickly).

I look forward to hearing from Dr. Morrow of the testimony's that will come from **"The Things that Make Men Cry."** This book will begin a revolution of change in all aspects of the community, the country and the world. The time is now. Let's do this...lives are depending on us.

Amazed by His Grace,

Bishop Eddie L. Long

INTRODUCTION

A young couple came to counseling to try to save their marriage of three years. The wife (Janet) painted a very vivid picture of the couple's drowning marriage, and she had no problem in articulating the issues that seemed to plague them. However, her husband (John) was very silent during sessions. So in my attempt to understand the underlying issues that negatively impacted this beautiful couple's chances of experiencing marital bliss, I asked each of them to come in for an individual session. I thought it necessary for each of them to be given the opportunity to discuss their individual issues without the other present. It is my belief that there are no bad marriages; rather there are impaired individuals whose unresolved personal issues contaminate and destroy the marriage.

The other motivation for seeing the couple separately was to give John an opportunity to express himself more freely, especially since he always had so little to say with his wife present. One spouse's commitment to remain silent during the therapy session may be attributed to his or her desire to avoid a heated argument that could very well erupt and last until the next session. I could sense that there was a lot John wanted and needed to talk about, but somehow he didn't have the words when the two of them were together.

After our normal greeting and exchange of pleasantries, I explained once again why I asked him to come alone. By the look on his face, I could tell that John had been thinking about our session, so I asked him what he wanted to talk about. I can still remember this strikingly distinguished looking gentleman sitting across from me in dead silence for what seemed like minutes. I decided to sit with him in his silence.

The only noise was the sound of a large clock ticking on the wall and just as I was about to check in with him, it happened. The tears began to well up in John's eyes, and then it was as if the flood gates swung wide open. The tears rolled down his face, and he began to sob uncontrollably. Since crying can be very healing, I waited a few moments before extending the conveniently placed box of tissue to him. John accepted it, pulled one out and attempted to dry his eyes, but the tears just would not stop.

I began to feel John's pain with every attempt he made to stop the tears. He was beyond the point of embarrassment. I think he had simply exposed a part of himself that had been carefully tucked away and hidden until that day, at least publicly. When John finally composed himself, he began to share his thoughts and feelings.

John reported that he was very much in love with his wife, but felt he was no match for her when it came to resolving conflicts. He explained that every time he attempted to share his concerns with Janet, she was able to articulate things better than he could, leaving him in a state of frustration and confusion. In other words, Janet was a much better debater than John. He was not even aware of the impact these hidden feelings had on his personal health and well-being, and his marriage.

Furthermore, John was even more unaware of the impact of his parents and their relationship on him and the way he engaged with his wife. For example, John's father was very quiet in the home, and when discussions and differences of opinion occurred between his parents, John's father would quickly retreat. It was easy to detect that John responded similarly to his wife, which was a learned response that he picked up from his family environment.

John had been crying silent tears for a long time, and because of his inner pain, his response was to withhold the love from the love of his life. His demeanor in the couple's sessions was characteristic of his demeanor at home, and his inability to effectively communicate with her caused him to simply stop talking to his bride. Janet interpreted his behavior to mean that he no longer loved her. She perceived him as cold, heartless, and distant, and was preparing herself for the worst case scenario, divorce.

After further assessment, I detected that John was suffering from a depressive disorder. According to the recent research, depression affects more than 6 million men in the United States. Unfortunately, the percentage is probably much higher because men tend to avoid seeking help for mental health issues. Rather, men suffer in silence and cry silent tears. It is for this reason that a greater understanding of the emotional world of men is essential, as well as the things that make men cry.

To complicate matters, females may not fully understand men's emotional make-up and are sometimes lacking in their ability and skills to respond to them in appropriate ways. Females also may hold negative attitudes and perceptions about men (some deserved and some undeserved). I was watching an old episode of the hit sitcom "**Living Single**," and Sinclair said to Kadisha, "Did you ever stop to think about what the world would be like without men? Kadisha, in her naturally humorous state replied, "A bunch of fat happy women without crime." While spoken in jest, men are viewed in a negative light, and they are often credited with making life miserable for women. Unfortunately, many good men who are suffering in silence from emotional pain are often misunderstood and labeled as aggressive and mean.

In our private time together, John revealed some of the things that made him cry, which serves as the impetus for this book "**The Things that Make Men Cry**." John had been crying silent tears for most of his life because of his experiences as a son, father, husband, employee, and as a man. As he talked about failed relationships with his present wife and young child from a previous marriage, past issues with his father and mother, stressors on the job, and his own fears and concerns, it was evident that John was suffering from emotional pain, which then led to more serious psychological distress.

The individual sessions with John proved to be very helpful in allowing him to discuss what was hurting him, and to properly address his depressive disorder. Individual therapy and marriage counseling gave this couple the opportunity to explore their individual issues, while helping them to really become acquainted with each other, and to gain more empathy and sensitivity to each other's needs.

In **"The Things that Make Men Cry,"** 14 courageous men share their thoughts about the complexities of manhood, and the pain associated with childhood issues, including the absence of fathers and early responsibilities placed on them as young boys growing up in single female headed households or in homes where fathers were present, yet still absent.

"The Things that Make Men Cry" also discusses the impact of failed love relationships, separation from children, the inability to understand and meet the emotional needs of the women they love, experiences of racism and discrimination, workplace and societal issues, financial struggles, hidden fears, and dreams deferred on men's overall well-being.

These men will speak about their silent tears and their reasons for failing to expose their emotional side to anyone.

"The Things that Make Men Cry" is first and foremost to promote a greater understanding of the emotional side of men and to validate their often silent pain. Some women fail to understand the pain men experience when they have unresolved issues from the past, the loss of wives and children due to death or divorce, or the loss of a job making them unable to provide for their family.

For example, John's story was extremely important in helping me to understand the root of his problems. But more important, John's story was helpful to his wife, because she was able to gain a greater understanding of her husband's pain and inner turmoil. Janet was able to develop empathy for her husband, which had been a very different concept for her to grasp in the past.

Second, **"The Things that Make Men Cry"** has been written to help men to become more aware of the negative consequences of untreated depression and other psychological disorders. This often hidden acknowledgment will help men to seek professional help before they become emotionally bankrupt and impaired.

Third, **"The Things that Make Men Cry"** will provide the rationale for the importance of men seeking a closer relationship with God, gaining positive role models, engaging in the process of ongoing self-development, building a strong family, and discovering their purpose and mission, all for the purpose of living a healthier purpose-focused lifestyle.

Fourth, **"The Things that Make Men Cry"** has been written to give men permission to express their feelings openly and honestly. Throughout the pages of this book, great men in the Bible, including our Lord and Savior Jesus Christ expressed their pain, sorrow, and grief through tears. Their feelings will be highlighted to help men to begin to feel more comfortable about allowing their emotional wounds to be revealed and ultimately healed.

Finally, it is my hope and prayer that hurting men all over the world will find this book as a guide to help them to acknowledge their pain, so they can begin their healing process.

God has a wonderful plan for each of your lives, and your participation in your inner healing will allow you to begin to live the life that God has intended for you to live.

This book is NOT intended to excuse men from taking responsibility for destructive behaviors targeted towards themselves, their women, their children, and others who love and care about them because of their inability to respond to and appropriately cope with their emotional pain. But I am prayerful that women will gain a greater understanding of the world and culture of men.

As a female author, I am quite humbled and honored to attempt to provide an understanding of the emotional side of men. However, the voices of the men interviewed for this timely project and others I have had the privilege of working with, as well as the current research, must be credited for providing the critical information needed to foster that understanding.

The participants of this project consisted of 14 males, who were primarily African American, ranging from 18-86 years of age, coming from diverse economic backgrounds, with the majority of them coming from middle income families. All of the men identified themselves as Christian, and with the exception of two, all were married. The men interviewed for this project were representative of a convenience sample who responded to a set of open-ended structured interview questions.

While the thoughts and feelings shared by the 14 men interviewed for this project are highlighted, it is important to note that their voices cannot be generalized to represent the voices of the entire male population. However, their participation in this project can help us to gain keen insight into the possible manner in which men respond to the issues they are confronted with on a daily basis. Further, this book will reflect the voices of hundreds of men I have been blessed to work with throughout my career as a psychologist.

Blessings and peace,

Dr. Gloria Morrow

PART I

∞

SHAPED INTO MANHOOD

Chapter 1

∞

What is a Man Anyway?

In God's economy, real men pray, real men open up to friends, real men cherish their
wives and love their children, real men kneel at the Cross. T.D. Jakes

George sat in my office looking as though the wind had been knocked out of him. After a lengthy dialogue in session, Mary looked George dead in the eyes and said these words: You are not a man! At first, George appeared to be thinking about his rebuttal to the harsh accusations made by his wife, but he quickly slumped back into his chair and once again became silent. In fact, he refused to speak until I quickly intervened to help the couple to become engaged in the session. When George did speak he asked his wife this question: What is a man anyway?

The issue of manhood is very important in gaining an understanding about men and the way they think, feel, and behave. People hold different views about what constitutes manhood. Therefore, I thought it important to first provide a working definition of manhood, both from a biological perspective as well as a social constructionist perspective because of its importance to this discussion.

One's perceptions and beliefs surrounding the role and responsibilities associated with manhood are important to discuss because men's silent suffering many times is the result of being unable to fulfill the social and cultural definition of manhood due to issues; such as financial constraints, divorce, grief and loss issues, racism and discrimination, incarceration, lack of education, domestic violence, psychological issues, such as depression, anxiety, PTSD (Post Traumatic Stress Disorder), or physical illness.

While this book is not intended primarily for an African American audience, the majority of the participants of this project are representatives from the African American community therefore, it is important to discuss them in more detail.

From the biological perspective, manhood is based on physical attributes such as features, appearances, strengths, etc. In the book, **"Black Man Emerging,"** White and Cone (1991) assert that biological manhood is based on physical attributes, sexuality, and the ability to reproduce (p. 255). However, when looking at the social and perhaps cultural definition of manhood, it is important to understand the impact of social norms and expectations that are placed on men within the social and cultural context. For example, White stated:

> *Social manhood, in an African American context, requires learning to be disciplined, competent, responsible, and aware of the history and ethics of Black people; it also means setting long-range goals that require persistent effort and making the commitment to uplifting oneself, family and community (p. 255).*

The inability to successfully meet the requirements of manhood can lead to feelings of depression and destructive self-medicating behaviors, such as drinking, drugs, affairs, and gambling. When men are unable to live up to family, community, and society's expectations of manhood, they may also experience feelings of frustration and self-disgust which can be taken out on those they love the most. When asked how it feels to be unable to support one's family, Donnie, a participant of this project stated: "It keeps you down and depressed." Unlike some other ethnicities, Black men are not only responsible for their family they are also responsible for the whole race.

What Does it Mean to be a Black Man?

In the profound book, **"Being a Black Man,"** Pulitzer Prize winner, Edward P. Jones cites Mayor Marc Morial, the former mayor of New Orleans who shared his response to this important question:

> *Black men relate to each other in a special way. It's the cohesion that comes from knowing, whatever your situation in life, you're carrying a special burden: But also that you're strong enough to carry it. Whatever they put on you, you can handle it. You can knock me down but I'm getting up. You can't knock me down with no love tap.*

Once again, the definition of manhood tends to depend on many factors, which explains why men may define themselves differently. The participants of this project were no exception to that diversity, and you will find a summary of their thoughts regarding the definition of manhood.

PARTICIPANTS' DEFINITION OF MANHOOD

- *A Real Man is the head of his household.*
- *He is a leader, who is helpful and considerate, especially to his wife and children.*
- *A man is a provider and protector of his family.*
- *A man is trustworthy, forthright, honest, and dependable.*

A man is one who keeps his word. When you say you are going to do something, you must do it. A man will not always be perfect about keeping his word, but in my opinion a good man keeps his word. Nate

- *A man is kind and loving, sensitive, yet strong; with the ability to balance the two.*
- *A man is STRONG. He is a person who leads and guides.*
- *A man knows who he is and uses those abilities to make things work for his wife and family. His strength helps him to lead.*
- *A man is able to hold his own ground, take care of the family, and hold a job.*
- *A man has to rescue others.*
- *A man should be the breadwinner of the house.*

Rev. Phillips, the eldest participant shared that in addition to being the head and supporter of the family, *"A man should be an example for his family. But most of all, he should be loving and kind."*

> *A man is accountable for his actions. A real man recognizes when he is right and when he is wrong. He can deal with the responsibility of fixing it or whatever action or punishment that goes with it. He can stand up and take it. Leonard*

Steven discussed the complexities associated with attempting to define manhood, especially in this modern day where many males are raised in single female headed households with few, if any real male role models to follow. This participant who himself was raised in such a family composition where his mother worked outside the home in a professional capacity had something quite different to contribute to this subject.

> *So many people have attempted to define manhood, some qualified and some not. But I guess for me, being a man is like being a woman. Knowing your roles and responsibilities whatever they are, because a man could be responsible for taking care of the home while his wife is at work."*

For men who hold more contemporary views on this topic, they may experience less stress if their women are considered the breadwinner. Remember, one's understanding of manhood is based more on one's social and cultural perspective than on biology. Further, the men who may shed the most tears around this issue are those who hold more traditional views of manhood because they may see themselves as a failure in their role as men. Also, men who espouse traditional manhood roles may have a difficult time adjusting to women who are more contemporary and independent in their thinking.

Some women believe it is easy for men to break their promises. For some men, that assumption may be true. However, a real man may be silently suffering because he has not only disappointed his woman, but he has disappointed himself and those who have imposed this important value on him.

In many of the definitions of manhood, one of the essential characteristics of manhood is Strength. No matter what, even when he is feeling weak and vulnerable, a man must be strong. Furthermore, he always has to wear the mask of strength and it is sometimes difficult for him to discuss his true feelings of fear, sadness, disappointment, and/or guilt with anyone, especially the important women in his life. He simply cannot let her know that he is feeling afraid or hurt. Many times, women are not allowed into their men's secret emotional world, and when they press to get in, men can become even more emotionally disconnected.

A few years ago, my father's oldest sister became ill and was hospitalized. Aunt Dora was unmarried, so she looked to my father to help her make important decisions. During the course of her illness, the time came when my father was asked to make the decision for her to have surgery. Dad agreed to the surgery because Aunt Dora only had a small chance of survival with or without it. He believed, and rightfully so, that if the surgery could give her any chance of survival whatsoever it was worth exercising that option. Unfortunately, Aunt Dora did not survive the surgery. Months later, my mother told me that dad was not himself. Even though he maintained his customary strong exterior, the person who was closest to him [my mom] knew he was not doing well.

I decided to talk to my father and through our conversation I learned that he was holding himself somewhat responsible for Aunt Dora's death because he signed for her to have the surgery. Thankfully, our conversation seemed to help him to share his thoughts and feelings, and to grieve appropriately over the loss of his sister. This example underscores the burden associated with men's understanding of what constitutes real manhood.

WHO TEACHES MEN ABOUT MANHOOD?

While society must bear its fair share of the responsibility for influencing the manhood process, one's socialization experiences in homes, cultural enclaves, and vital institutions must also be credited as a significant influential component.

There are a variety of critical players who help to develop men's concept of manhood. According to Steven, one of the participants of this project:

There were four people who actually influenced my thinking about manhood. The first one is my grandfather who taught me and showed me that a man should be a source of stability. My mother taught me that a man is kind, respectful, gentle, and loving. Next, my biological father taught me through his absence and bad behavior, that a man should be reliable and someone you can count on. Then my step-father taught me that you should go after what you want in life.

The majority of the participants learned about manhood from fathers and grandfathers. However, a few of them had a strong maternal influence, which most certainly impacted the way they viewed the roles and responsibilities held by men. Pastor Tommy discussed his mother's influence on his early indoctrination into manhood:

I learned how to be a man from my mother. My mother was a real man. She did it all. She was smart, intellectual, down to earth, a visionary, and she had a way with people. My daddy taught me how to go to work and bring my money home, but my mother taught me how to take care of the things that needed to be taken care of.

Berkeley also discussed his experiences with his mother:

My mother played a very significant role in our socialization. She was the one who went out into the community and participated in a lot of social activities. She was also very prominent in the church and kept us involved in that spirit for all of our lives. We had to participate in church activities. She was what was known as an outreach person for the church and we had to accompany her to visit the sick and prepare meals for those who needed food. There was one significant thing she taught us. There were no special roles for men. There was equality in the house. There were three boys and three girls and we had to do everything that could be done in the house, such as cooking, washing and mending our own clothes. So she was a little ahead of her time as a feminist.

Even though Berkeley's mother did not follow the traditional role expectations of the day, some of the roles were consistent with the ones we are most familiar with as it relates to men. Berkeley further shared:

My father was the one who went out and did all the work and brought home the money. Boys were taught how to work and make money. My mom was a seamstress in the community. We also baked and made cakes for weddings as gifts and as an opportunity to make money. We had a small farm and my dad was the one who sort of played the leadership role there. He was an engineer by trade, but when it came to looking after the animals, I was the one who did most of that.

Vernon's experiences were similar to those of Berkeley:

I grew up in the real south and therefore had a lot of influences during my growth as a young boy. My mother and father contributed to my growth into manhood and leadership, but my father was my greatest influence. He showed me what a man's role was and I watched him put it into action.

Nonetheless, most of the participants' understanding about manhood came from close male figures.

> *My father taught me to stand up and be a man and try to do right by life and my family. Donnie*

Rob shared, "*I believe I became a man by observing my father's image. My father's image was a man of very strong character. He was a man who was honest in his feelings. He was very compassionate and patient.*

The early messages boys receive in their home and community environments impact their understanding of and perhaps their indoctrination into manhood. However, it is important to note that some of the things men learn about manhood early on are tested, tried, and modified due to new experiences, both positive and negative, and the culture in which they are raised.

Each of the men who participated in this project acknowledged that who they are as men has been highly influenced by fathers, mothers, wives, grandparents, and primary caregivers. However, one of the most influential teachers on the topic of manhood, and every topic for that matter, is Jesus Christ, our Lord and Savior. He was and continues to be the perfect example of both man and God. Tommy S. reflected on the role of Christ in his development into manhood.

> *The Bible says when you become a man, you put away childish things, and I am still growing every day. Every day is a new adventure. I have a purpose. In the past, I was a taker. It was all about me. I was selfish, filled with pride. I was all about fulfilling myself. But now I have learned that a man is a giver, and when you give it shall be given back to you. A Christian man is a priest. He provides for his wife, and he makes sure she gets what she needs. Through Christ, I have learned how to be a better husband, lover, friend, father, and grandfather. I know who I am.*

A Real Man knows who God is and walks in relationship with Him, because God is the one who created man. Philip

WHAT IS A GODLY MAN?

According to 2 Timothy 3:10-17, a Godly man follows the doctrine of Christ, lives a Godly lifestyle, knows his purpose and walks in it, has faith, is long suffering, demonstrates love and perseverance, is willing to suffer persecution, and lives by the Word of God so that he may be complete and thoroughly equipped for every Good work.

In 2 Timothy 3:2-9, **GODLY MEN ARE NOT ...** a lover of themselves, lovers of money, boasters, proud, blasphemers, disobedient to parents, unthankful, unholy, unloving, unforgiving, slanderers, without self-control, brutal, despisers of God, traitors, headstrong, haughty, lovers of pleasure rather than lovers of God, those who have a form of godliness but denying its power, those who are constantly learning, but never coming to the knowledge of the truth. Ungodly men will never progress because their folly will be manifest to all.

Men who harbor emotional baggage are highly at risk of developing the characteristics of an ungodly man. These characteristics will be damaging to men and their family and friends. Those who lack Godly examples of what a man is supposed to be and do may be poorly equipped for manhood. Further, they may not possess the Spiritual wisdom to positively impact the lives of the boys and men God has entrusted in their care.

Chapter 2

∞

Big Boys Don't Cry

Tears are the liquid cleanser that helps to wash away the stuff you are going through.
Steven Wayne

The lessons learned about manhood have shaped and continue to shape men's thoughts, feelings, and behaviors towards themselves, the women in their lives, their children, the community, and perhaps the world. For example, men who have been taught the traditional definition of manhood through both observations and formal and informal lessons may have also been taught that it is not okay for a man to cry.

These lessons are learned very early in life. Philip shared one of the early lessons he learned about crying:

I never saw my father cry. Nate

When I was coming up, my brother always told me, Don't Cry! Don't ever let anybody see you defeated. Don't ever let anybody see your weaknesses. I grew up with the mindset that a man is not supposed to cry, he's not supposed to show his feelings. When you turn on the TV that's all you hear and see, the hardness in men. I definitely think that the world makes it hard for men to express themselves, and I am still learning how to communicate properly, and learning how to discuss my feelings.

HOW DO MESSAGES IN CHILDHOOD

IMPACT ONE'S ADULTHOOD?

The early messages children receive from those they love and respect have a strong impact on shaping their adult lives. Therefore, if a male child is taught that crying is a sign of weakness, especially when he reaches adulthood it is very possible for him to walk around in pain and suffering without telling anyone.

Rob reflected on his thoughts and feelings related to men's display of emotions:

John the beloved disciple of Christ laid his head on Jesus' breast and showed tenderness at the Last Supper. His Savior was going away. Most men are afraid. We're taught to be macho, and to stand up and be strong. So we get our tattoos, and we get buff, but when we lay up with our wives, we don't know how to talk. Men talk about business, but most men don't know how to lie in their wife's arms. Sometimes I need it. When I get home, I need to lie in my wife's arms and tell her, I feel like giving up, or I'm tired today. You know, my kids are doing this, and things are not going right. And sometimes, I just need to cry, but we have been taught not to cry. If you cry, you are a sissy.

In support of Rob's conclusions, I have a story of my own to share. I was just a young child when I heard a conversation between my uncle and his young son that sticks with me to this day. My cousin ran into the house after being beaten up by the neighborhood bully. Tears were running down his face as he flew into the arms of his father. I did not understand the dynamic that had just occurred because I was a child, but in looking back as an adult, I believe my cousin was waiting to hear the kind of comforting words his mother would routinely give, such as "come over here baby, and tell mama what happened." My feisty aunt would have dried his eyes, kissed him where it hurt, and then she would have stormed out of the house to have a friendly chat with the perpetrator's parents.

My cousin did not receive words of comfort. Rather, my uncle moved his young son away from him, looked him sternly in the eyes and said these words: "Boy hush that crying. **BIG BOYS DON'T CRY**. Wipe those eyes and go back out there. If that boy hits you again, you'd better hit him back or don't come back in here to tell me about it." My uncle went one step further and told my cousin if he did not stand up for himself, he was going to get it when he came home. I can assure you that my young cousin learned that it was not okay for a man to cry.

It is important to add, however, that crying physical tears does not imply that men are able to express their innermost thoughts and feelings in a way that promotes good emotional health and well-being. Nor does it guarantee that men will have good relationships with women with open communication and intimacy. In fact, it is safe to say that even though tears may well up in a man's eyes when he is sad, or moved to do so, long after the tears have dried, he continues to sob in silence because he has not been given permission to open himself up in a way that makes him feel vulnerable and weak.

Of course, there are exceptions to every rule, but men are particularly less likely to talk about deeply felt hurt and sorrow in the way most women do. Men may be crying on the outside, but those tears may not be an accurate reflection of what is really going on for them on the inside.

My cousin was certainly not the only male child to matriculate through Manhood Training 101. Some of the participants of this project shared their thoughts on this subject. Most of the men agreed that they were taught that crying was not okay, especially those who were between the ages of 45-85.

According to Leonard,

I probably was taught that it was not okay to cry, and I lived by my father's motto. I don't think my kids would ever see me cry. My wife has probably seen me cry once in the ten or twelve years we have been together. I am a very internal person. I swallow things up and deal with them. For me, crying means I am just lost and don't know what else to do. As a man you want to be strong. So crying basically says I can't deal with it, and it shows everybody else around that I can't deal with it.

Men today have been taught not to cry, to hold in your feelings because crying is a sign of weakness. Tommy Stewart

Pastor Tommy had this to say on the subject:

> *I was taught that men don't cry, you just suck it up. So the thing that makes you want to cry, if you think about it before you actually do the act, as a man you won't do it. Sometimes the emotion comes upon you so quickly that you find yourself crying. Then, when the mind engages you, all of a sudden you try to compose yourself. It is so funny to watch men who become emotional. The first thing they say is, Oh I'm sorry, excuse me, I am emotional.*

Rev. Phillips discussed the difficulty in men shedding tears, which supports the traditional definition of manhood. Somehow strength and tears just don't go well together.

> *It has been a hard thing for me to cry as a man. By being a minister, I always try to hold back tears in order to support those that I come into contact with. It is not a wise thing to go to try to help someone with tears in your eyes. You have to be stronger than that, if you are minister. I do not remember ever seeing my father cry.*

Many have begun to accept that crying is a natural and healthy emotion, especially after traumatic and life changing experiences with those they love and care about. For example, Berkeley stated: *"Yes, it is okay for a man to cry. As a matter of fact, my mom taught me that crying was something we should not be ashamed of. She wanted us to know that men were to be strong, but crying was fine."* Even though this mother gave her sons permission to cry, it was tempered with the notion that you must be strong.

Yes, it is definitely okay for a man to cry. I think that a true man can cry because when you don't cry you actually deny your humanity.
Philip

Even though some men say it is okay to cry, are they really getting everything out that is necessary to live a healthy lifestyle? While many of the participants acknowledged that tears may be healthy for today's man, there was still the sense that there is no real outlet for men to share what those tears represent.

I was talking to a man who lost a child due to a debilitating disease. During the time funeral arrangements were being made, the child's mother was overcome with grief, and was having a very difficult time accepting her son's death. The father continued to go to work and kept going as if nothing happened. His response to his young son's death was more than his wife could handle, and while in a period of irrational thinking due to her emotional condition, the wife accused her husband of not caring that their son had died. This grief stricken wife and mother was expecting her husband to respond similarly to her. Sadly, her husband's non-emotional response to his son's death became a great source of contention in the couple's already tumultuous marriage.

In session with this man some 15 years after the death of his son, he began to weep uncontrollably, and he expressed great relief in being able to finally cry about losing his son. He remarked,

"I simply could not break down in front of my wife. My job was to be strong and take care of her and my other children. I had to keep going. I just could not break down, even though it felt as if my heart was torn right into pieces. I just never had the opportunity to grieve, and I still miss him to this very day."

These differences in the way men and women express their emotions and deal with pain can be the source of many misunderstandings. It can also lead to divorce for those marriages that are already fragile.

IMPACT OF UNEXPRESSED FEELINGS

When males do not have a healthy outlet by which to share and express what they are thinking and feeling, they are more vulnerable to mental and physical illnesses, and they sometimes become violent. It is important to understand that males have been traumatized and victimized just as women have. However, women are much better at expressing their thoughts and feelings, even if they find solace in sister friends and family members who may not be healthy enough to help them.

Male conversations can sometimes be superficial. They tend to swap success stories because of their competitive nature. Rarely do they discuss their feelings of vulnerability and fear, or feelings of hurt and pain with each other in the same way women do.

The point worth noting here is, women have an emotional valve with a release button that is begging to be activated. Since males have been socialized to repress their feelings at all costs to maintain an appearance of strength, many men harbor anger, bitterness, hurt and guilt feelings causing them to suffer from depression and anxiety. Depression is often viewed as anger turned inward. Therefore, sad and frustrated men might lash out in violence in response to the pain they are experiencing on the inside. It is as though they are walking around with a pressure cooker that is just waiting to blow.

NOTE: The aforementioned conclusions are in **NO** way intended to excuse acts of violence perpetrated towards women. Rather, they are simply to bring about a greater understanding of the potential impact of unexpressed feelings of hurt and pain.

THERE IS MORE ROOM OUT THAN IN

After years of failed relationships, including three marriages ending in divorce, Aaron thought it important for him to seek individual therapy to help him figure out what he was doing wrong in the relationship department. As customary in my work with clients, I asked him to paint a picture as vivid or discrete as he felt comfortable about what his life was like as a child.

Throughout the course of four sessions, Aaron unpeeled more and more of the traumatic layers of his horrid childhood. He shared his early recollections of child sexual and physical abuse between the ages of five and nine perpetrated by both his mother and her boyfriend.

When he began to act out sexually with a 12-year old girl in the girl's bathroom at school, the teacher who discovered them had the foresight to interview him and he revealed what was going on at home. Aaron and his five siblings were removed from the family home, and his mother and her boyfriend were arrested.

At the age of ten, he began his career as a foster child. Aaron recalled being very angry, especially with females and was moved from foster home to foster home, and eventually landed in a group home until his 18th birthday. By the 10th grade, however, he decided to participate in his education and after graduating from high school, he enrolled at the local community college and moved in with an older sister.

Aaron reported having a very difficult time getting along with women because of the anger and unresolved issues he continued to harbor against his mother. He was also very sad, and until those weeks in therapy, Aaron had never uttered a word to anyone (other than the elementary school teacher) about his past.

While in foster care, he saw several therapists, (mostly female) and he stated, "I only told them what I wanted them to know." This deception helped him to earn the reputation of an angry and avoidant male. Aaron walked around crying silent tears for most of his young life because of his emotional need to dismiss his feelings. Because of his experiences with women, he generalized his views of the few women he had negative encounters with to ALL women.

Living in an abusive home also impacts men and women's love relationships. When attempting to engage in love relationships with females, Aaron always found himself detached, unresponsive, angry, and combative (both verbally and physically). Also, men's views about love relationships and marriage can be negative when they witness mothers being physically abused.

Leonard recalls watching his mother being abused by his father:

The only thing I took home from that is to really love your kids because she endured everything my father put her through because of us. We were so young. We would tell mom to just leave him, but she would say, No, No No. She wanted us to have a father, so she took the abuse so we would have a father. That just showed me what I didn't want to do in life if I was in a relationship that wasn't working. I think that's what took me so long to actually get married. We lived together for five years before getting married because I was so unsure about getting married because of everything I had been through."

Men do suffer from the impact of childhood violence and trauma, either as a victim of the violence, or as a witness to the violence. These traumatic events may influence men to either repeat the cycle of violence or to become totally passive and disengaged. Failure to acknowledge and confront maladaptive thoughts and feelings will leave one feeling depressed and anxious, and more vulnerable to uncontrollable anger and rage.

By the end of my time with Aaron, he had become much more open and he expressed feelings of relief. I asked him what helped him the most during our time together, and he replied: *"I learned that there is more room out than in. It was time to get that poison out of my system so I could live."*

REAL MEN DO CRY

Not only do men have a difficult time expressing their feelings openly with their women and others in their lives, some have a difficult time opening up to God through prayer and supplication. It is important to note that strong men in the Bible dealt with some of the same issues that men deal with today. They experienced pain, grief, and sorrow. In fact, these **REAL MEN** cried **REAL TEARS**.

In the Book of Psalms, David openly acknowledged his feelings of guilt, sadness, fear, and anger. His willingness to expose himself in that way was and continues to be important today. Macho men may have a difficult time confessing wrongdoing, or to even use words in their prayers that suggest the very notion of fear or apprehension. When David was experiencing intense feelings of fear and sadness, he cried out to the Lord. Let's visit Psalms 6.

O Lord, do not rebuke me in Your anger, nor chasten me in Your hot displeasure. Have mercy on me, O Lord, for I am weak; O Lord, heal me, for my bones are troubled. My soul also is greatly troubled; But you, O Lord-how long? Return, O Lord, deliver me! Oh, save me for Your mercies' sake! For in death there is no remembrance of You; In the grave who will give You thanks? I am weary with my groaning; All night I make my bed swim; I drench my couch with my tears. My eye wastes away because of grief; It grows old because of all mine enemies. Depart from me, all you workers of iniquity; For the Lord has heard the voice of my weeping. The Lord has heard my supplication; The Lord will receive my prayer. Let all my enemies be ashamed and greatly troubled; Let them turn back and be ashamed suddenly.

Although David was a strong King who as a young boy killed Goliath, he acknowledged his area of weakness, and asked for God's mercy and help.

Jesus Christ was also acquainted with grief, not only because of his pending death at the hands of evil and unrighteous men, but he grieved with those He loved. You may recall in the 11th Chapter of the book of John that Jesus was summoned to the home of Mary and Martha because their brother Lazarus was sick. Even though Jesus loved this faithful family, He did not respond immediately.

There are a variety of interpretations of this text to explain Jesus' delay. Some say He may have been delayed because of the large crowds He encountered en route to the home of Mary and Martha. However, the popular belief is that Jesus already knew that Lazarus would live and He wanted to strengthen the faith of Mary and Martha and others who needed to have their faith activated and/or renewed.

However, Lazarus did die and was buried before Jesus arrived on the scene. When Jesus arrived, He found Mary overcome with grief.

> *When Jesus therefore saw her weeping, and the Jews also weeping which came with her, He groaned in the Spirit, and was troubled, and said, where have ye laid him? They said unto Him, Lord, come and see. Jesus wept.*
> *John 11:33-35*

Although Jesus knew the end of the story, He displayed a human emotional response to the situation openly before others to see. It appears He was filled with compassion, sorrow, and maybe even disappointment that the faith of Mary and Martha was not as strong as He would have liked it to be.

The point of this powerful text here is to remind men everywhere, that regardless to what you have learned throughout your lifetime Jesus invites you to open up that side of yourself that has been boarded up too long. Perhaps, that is what is needed for men to be more open to the love of Jesus Christ, and to enter into real relationship with Him more easily.

In fact, if you really want to see God move on your behalf, you'd better cry out to Him.   Exodus 2: 23-25 states: *"Now it happened in the process of time that the king of Egypt died.   Then the children of Israel groaned because of the bondage, and they cried out: and their cry came up to God because of the bondage.   So God heard their groaning, and God remembered His covenant with Abraham, with Isaac, and with Jacob.   And God looked upon the children of Israel, and God acknowledged them."*

In the words of the great hymn of the church:

I love the Lord, He heard my cry and pitied every groan. Long as I live and trouble rise, I'll hasten to His throne.

Chapter 3

∞

Mama's Little Man

Women can only raise a boy to be a man just like mama. Tommy Morrow

Manhood can occur prematurely, especially when a man is not in the home due to separation, divorce, or death. Some boys are forced to take on the role of a man much too early, and that role can be exploited by well meaning mothers who are not only in need of help with the other children, but in desperate need of male presence and companionship.

MARY'S LITTLE MAN

Jesus felt a strong sense of responsibility towards His mother Mary which may have resulted from the fact that the last mention in Scripture of his earthly father Joseph was when Jesus was 12 years old. This may imply that Mary lived as a single mother after that time, and even though Jesus was about His Father's business throughout the earth, he was still concerned about and obligated to His mother.

When Jesus went to the cross, he knew the importance of assigning someone to care for His mother. The job was assigned to

John as these powerful words were spoken by Jesus on the cross, first to His mother: *"Woman behold your son!"* and then to John: *Behold your mother!* John 19:26-27. Jesus was instructing John to take care of His mother, and He was instructing His mother to accept John as her son.

So it is not unusual that some men commit themselves to taking care of mothers who have no other man to care for them, or those who have men who are non-functional in the home. However, this great obligation if not entered into in a balanced and healthy way can prove to be destructive.

FORCED TO GROW UP TOO SOON

On Walter's 6th birthday, his biological father was killed on his way home from work. The family was devastated. Walter had 2 younger siblings, but his mother began to rely on him as the replacement man of the house. By the time Walter was in middle school, he provided care for his young sisters. When the girls began to date, it was Walter who issued the warning to their nervous dates to bring the girls safely home before their curfew. Walter also became his mother's constant companion, as she never remarried, and it is not surprising that he got a job as soon as he could get a permit to help support the family.

Some of the participants could relate to Walter's story because they too lost their fathers because of death. Rev. Phillips recalled his father dying when he was only 10 years old.

"Even though I had older brothers, somehow I became the man of the house. Long after the death of my mother, I continued to help support my siblings and their families out of a sense of responsibility."

Other participants shared what it was like to step into their father's shoes because of separation or divorce. Tommy S. stated:

I didn't have a good role model as a father. My father left my mother at an early age, and at the age of five years old, I had to break into the bathroom to prevent my mother from committing suicide several times. My mother would drag me out of bed when I was seven so I could walk with her as she looked for my father at 3 or 4 o'clock in the morning. Seeing my mother hurting over my father did a lot to me. I was the oldest of six kids, so I tried to be the little man, when I was just a boy. I had to grow up real fast, and I started stealing and doing bad things to satisfy my mother's pain and to help her provide for the family.

Tommy Stewart weighed in on the subject. "I grew up without a father. It was mom at home, and I was the one who stepped in to help support my sisters and brothers. At a young age, I had a lawn service so I could bring in money to support the family."

Nate became the **"Little Man"** because his dad left him in charge while he was away from home. Nate recalled:

"My father put me in charge of the household because he traveled a lot. He was a military officer plus, he was a Black man in the military trying to make a name for himself, which he finally did one day at everyone's expense. So I was around women a lot and I participated in raising my sisters."

At an early age, boys can develop an unhealthy alliance with their mothers that can severely impact their relationship with women in adulthood. Boys who become the man of the house tend to develop a serious sense of responsibility to take care of their mother in many aspects, making it difficult for girlfriends and wives to be given their proper place and position. However, this responsibility and duty can create grief for men because of their inability to please two women, both of whom they love.

This great sense of responsibility usually follows men throughout their lifetime, and they may continue to take care of the financial needs of their mother and/or siblings even when they cannot afford to maintain two homes. This often unintentional obligation can be problematic for husbands and wives who have not appropriately discussed and resolved these issues prior to marriage. Wives often feel like second classed citizens blaming their in-laws for interfering in their married lives, thus contributing to poor relationships between mother-in-laws and daughter-in-laws.

It is also important to note that mothers can sometimes prevent men from learning how to be a man from fathers when fathers are absent and mothers harbor animosity. Mothers may also disallow fathers to teach sons adequately even when the father is in the home. Be reminded that men and women are different, therefore, men approach parenting differently. While women can be more nurturing, caring, and compassionate, men can be consummate teachers and instructors. Some women still have a difficult time supporting men in their preferred parenting approaches and their interference can make it difficult for children to respect, obey, and learn important lessons from their father.

NOTE: It is very important for women to allow their sons' fathers to participate in their upbringing. The exception to this advice would be in cases where fathers are physically and/or sexually abusing their children. In those rare cases, it is critically important for mothers to remove their children from unsafe environments and to notify the appropriate authorities to further ensure the safety of themselves and their children.

Contrary to some reports, single mothers can and do raise healthy, respectful, and productive male children "as long as the children's needs for safety, emotional security, affection, and guidance are met," p. 205, White Cone, 1999. However, as often as possible, it is important for young men to have positive male role models in their lives, especially those fathers who want to be in the lives of their sons. A mother may only be able to teach her sons how to be a man just like mama.

Mothers sometimes get in the way of their sons' growth and development by not allowing them to grow up and stand on their own. In Matthew 20:20-28 you will hear a dialogue between a loving mother and Jesus Christ that demonstrates the aforementioned point.

Then the mother of Zebedee's sons came to Him with her sons, kneeling down and asking something from Him. And He said to her, 'What do you wish?' She said to Him, 'Grant that these two sons of mine may sit, one on Your right hand and the other on the left, in Your kingdom.' But Jesus answered and said, 'You do not know what you ask. Are you able to drink the cup that I am about to drink, and be baptized with the baptism that I am baptized with?' They said to Him, 'we are able.' So He said to them, 'You will indeed drink my cup, and be baptized with the baptism that I am baptized with, but to sit on My right hand and on My left is not Mine to give, but it is for those for whom it is prepared by My Father."

It was apparent that this mother had not taught her sons the importance of serving for the sake of serving because she had more than likely served them too much. Jesus used this opportunity to teach this family that there is greatness in serving even if you do not receive the reward you believe you deserve. Jesus created a teachable moment for this mother and her sons as well as the disgruntled onlookers who were upset because they believed these boys were going to receive something they did not deserve:

"But Jesus called them to Himself and said, 'You know that the rulers of the Gentiles lord it over them, and those who are great exercise authority over them. Yet it shall not be so among you, but whoever desires to become great among you, let him be your servant. And whoever desires to be first among you, let him be your slave, just as the Son of Man did not come to be served, but to serve, and to give His life a ransom for many.'"

This text illustrates the importance of teaching sons how real men should love God and serve Him, with no strings attached. For when one loves and serves God, one does not have a problem loving and serving others.

PART II

∞

THE THINGS THAT MAKE
MEN CRY

Chapter 4

∞

Open Wounds

Wounds will never heal unless they are acknowledged and treated ... Gloria Morrow

Have you ever had a nasty cut that you allowed to go untreated for a long time? I know you were taught to drench that cut with alcohol, peroxide, or some other antiseptic. Then you had to pour the liquid deep into the cut to prevent the likelihood that infections would occur and spread. People walk around with invisible wounds that have gone untreated for too long, causing infection to set in and spread throughout one's system. If you aren't careful, you may lose a limb because of your failure to properly treat a nasty cut.

Those nasty cuts may be invisible to the naked eye, but they are affecting you and everyone in your life. When we think about males in this society, especially Black males, we tend to have a difficult time removing the images that are often associated with the thoughts, feelings, and behaviors of males. One has only to look at the evening news, or read the local newspaper to get an image of society's impressions of men in this country.

Males are too often characterized as aggressive, violent, strong, criminal, cheater, perpetrator, thug, and the list goes on. Rarely are we given an inside look into the true emotional underpinnings of men and the things that make them hurt on the inside. The truth is, men are emotional beings and some are hurting and in pain because of their open wounds due to past traumas, abuses and abandonment issues.

Tommy S. talked about the negative things that were said to him when he was growing up that impacted him in negative ways. *"My mother would say to me, 'You're nothing... You're dumb, you're just like your father, and you're just like his brother.'"* Negative statements of this nature have the potential to cause children to grow up believing them, with the possibility of living out a self-fulfilling prophecy. When one sees oneself in a negative light, one will surely be moved to tears, both internally and externally.

Men also cry because of past mistakes. Sometimes it is difficult for men to forgive themselves for the mistakes they have made with regard to their wives, children, and even themselves. While I am in no way condoning or sanctioning adultery, men and women sometimes fall into adulterous situations because of their emotional/psychological condition. Therefore, do not assume that all men who get caught up in the infidelity trap are unrepentant and lack remorse and sadness because of their behavior. Many of them are very sorry that they hurt the woman they love.

To complicate matters, however, women promise to forgive and restore their husbands, but continue to bring up the other woman and the affair repeatedly. Since men are unable to engage in emotionally charged discussions the way women are, they may shut down emotionally and physically giving the impression they do not care about their wife's feelings, or they are really in love with the other woman. When men fail to forgive themselves old wounds may remain open. Also, when men feel they cannot be forgiven it makes matters even worse.

The participants of this project discussed 5 important factors that contribute to their silent tears the most: (1) Absent fathers, (2) Shattered dreams, (3) Love relationships, (4) Disconnection from children, and (5) Social injustice.

Your open wounds will never heal unless they are acknowledged and treated with the right medication. Jesus, our Lord and Savior could teach us some things about wounds and how to become healed. *"But He was wounded for our transgressions, He was bruised for our iniquities: for the chastisement of our peace was upon Him; and with His strips we are healed,"* Isaiah 53:5. Begin to look to Jesus for your healing.

IN THE SPACE PROVIDED BELOW, WRITE SOME OF THE THINGS THAT MAKE YOU CRY!

Chapter 5

∞

I Miss My Dad!

I am called to be a father to the fatherless… Bishop Eddie L. Long

Unfortunately, some males grow up without their biological fathers. This absence of fathers is due in part to divorce or death. In some cases, dad was never in the picture in the first place. Regardless to the reason, the absence of a father in the lives of males is hurtful and painful. If you really want to know the truth, this absence is also hurtful and painful for fathers who wanted the opportunity to raise their sons. Men who are unable to be in the lives of their children for whatever reason, good or bad, experience a serious loss on the inside, and in some cases they never recover from that loss.

Rev. Phillips who is now 89 years of age, reflects on what it was like when his father died prematurely.

My father was a good example for me. He displayed his duty as a father by taking care of his family. He was loving and kind to everyone in the family. He was a responsible man. But he died when I was just 10 years old. His death still hurts me and I am now an old man. I missed so much by him not being there, and I had to become the one who was responsible for the family. There was so much he didn't get time to teach me. It still hurts!

When fathers leave due to separation or divorce, boys sometimes experience feelings of rejection and abandonment. These negative feelings can contribute to boy's belief that there is something wrong with them. A boy's sense of identity is compromised because there is no reflection of him in the mirror which can come through positive interactions with dad. Even when the boy becomes a man, the little boy is still crying out for daddy on the inside, missing him and needing him, even though he may have sons and daughters of his own. Boys need their dads to teach them about life and to validate who they are. That is why they are constantly looking for their dad's attention and approval. Steven shared his feelings about the impact of the absence of his own father:

The absence of a real father has been the thing that has been a real tear jerker for me even as an adult. I've always been a person who longed for intimacy and relationship. Not having a real relationship with a father has been an interesting thing for me to go through."

Philip described how he responded to the absence of his father in the home: *"I think we cry a lot when we did not have a father growing up. I felt insecure as I tried to find my identity in a world where a false image of manhood is painted."*

Males living in the world without dads in their lives may experience inner sadness and pain that can easily turn into anger and rage toward their father or males in general. The bad behavior of one male can dictate the way sons view all males. Sometimes this negative perception of the way men are prevents males from having positive relationships with good yet imperfect males. Male relationships can sometimes be very superficial because of men's lack of experience with positive and nurturing male role models while growing up. This phenomenon may explain why some men are competitive by nature, and constantly seek bigger toys and gadgets, as opposed to building strong relationships.

Even I did not realize the impact of the absent father in the lives of males in my early adulthood. My biological son grew up without his father, and I thought that as long as I provided him with everything I thought he needed, and devoted my time and attention to him that he would be just fine. What I did not realize was the older he became, the more he saw himself as defective without a true sense of identity. I was in the bleachers for every game from elementary school through high school, took him every place imaginable, and was a devoted mother.

However, nothing could take away the pain he experienced because his father was missing in action. Some males erroneously believe that their father's absence is their fault. I was talking to a young man who shared his thoughts with me: "Maybe if I were smarter, nicer, or more handsome, maybe my dad would love me and he would not have left me."

Men who grew up with verbally and physically abusive men sometimes devote more quality time and attention to young men outside their homes because of the fear they will harm their own biological sons in the same way they were harmed.

MY DAD WAS IN THE HOME

In my work, I am constantly reminded that some men are hurt because of fathers who were in the home, yet absent. Ralph, a 22 year old male requested counseling to help him to deal with anger issues that were interfering with his job performance. While collecting the historical data, Ralph shared that his parents had been married for 25 years and were still married.

However, when asked about his relationship with his father he stated:

"We don't really have a relationship. When I was growing up, my father worked, and when he came home he rarely had time for us. I think he was ashamed that he was a day laborer with 6 children, and he pretended we were not there. My mother was our principle caretaker. All I can remember is waiting quietly outside for my dad to come home so I can get him to toss the baseball to me before nightfall. But it never happened! When he did say something, he was always fussing and snapping at us, like he hated us. Boy how I hated him, yet loved him at the same time. I just wanted him to love me back and pay some attention to me."

Ralph's story is not uncommon, because some men have been socialized to work and take care of the family leaving the parenting duties primarily to mothers. If men are not careful, they will behave in similar ways because that is all they have been exposed to. In other cases, women do not allow fathers to participate in the rearing of their sons. These mothers constantly interfere with fathers' attempts to discipline and engage with their sons.

Some fathers may not be emotionally or physically present because they are silently suffering from the lethal effects of untreated depression or other psychological disorders, causing them to isolate and withdraw from family members. See Chapter 10 for a fuller discussion of psychological disorders that may impact men.

Boys grow up resenting those fathers who were in the home, yet absent. They feel a sense of rejection and abandonment, and those feelings may be even stronger because their father was right there all the time. Ralph would say on a routine basis:

> *"I think I would have felt better if dad had never been in the home. What is one to think about someone who would come home after work, look at his children, and then flee to his bedroom and close the door behind him? What did that say about us? What was wrong with us? These are the questions that would run through my mind and they still do. I would really like my father to answer these questions one day."*

Men may become so involved in their work until their children are neglected. Children need more than their own room and all the video games they can play. THEY NEED THEIR DADS! Some professions make it more difficult for fathers to spend quality time with their children, such as pastors. They have the responsibility of taking care of their church family, which can often become the priority.

As a P.K. (Pastor's Kid) and a P.W. (Pastor's Wife) I have been blessed to be in the lives of two men who understood their primary responsibility was to their wife and children. Pastors that fail to place the needs of their family before the congregations they serve may develop poor relationships with wives and children who may become angry and bitter with the pastor, the church, and God. It is very sad when men focus all their energy and time on saving the world and lose their own family.

Some men still have open wounds because their father divorced their mother. In my work with clients, I sometimes ask these wounded sons to write letters they will never send to parents who have hurt them in order to assist them in their healing process. This assignment is to also help clients to begin the forgiveness process which is critical to their healing.

A young man wrote a letter to his father, and he has given me permission to share it with you. His letter demonstrates the type of pain that some boys experience and maintain well into adulthood when they lose their fathers after a brutal divorce.

LETTER TO MY DAD – (Unedited)

Hi Dad,

This is your little boy. I am writing this letter to try and explain to you about how I feel about the life you have given me and the relationship we have as father and son. First, I want to give credit where credit is due. I had a wonderful childhood and a loving home thanks to you and Mom. I grew up in a happy home, where you and Mom were married and lived your lives as an example for me to learn from and follow. Because of Mom's ethnicity, I had the privilege of being exposed to another culture. Because of you, I learned with it meant to be a man. Seeing you in your military uniform when you were younger made me want to be like you. Seeing you treat my Mom with love and adoration made me proud to call you my father. I always wanted to grow up and have the life, not to mention provide the same kind of life for myself and my family. I never doubted that I was wanted and loved by my parents. I was happy and viewed life through innocent and wondrous eyes. Life and the meaning of love held an element of magic for me. But then, when I was 14, you ended that world for me. I sat and watched as you and my Mom got divorced. I couldn't understand what was going on except that you were no longer in the house and that my family was falling apart. Although it was hard, I thought I was able to handle it because I was 14 and at first, it seemed that it was going to okay because you made noticeable efforts to spend time with me and let me know that it wasn't my fault and that you still loved me and Mom. That didn't last long though. You began to lie to me about gifts you supposedly bought me, started making excuses about why you didn't have time to spend with me, and started calling another woman and her children your wife and kids. How do you think that made me feel? I couldn't comprehend what I was hearing. You even tried to convince and make me call her Mom and her kid sister. They weren't my family. To me, they were responsible for destroying my family. Your actions conveyed to me that you chose them over us, over me. Why? I'm your flesh and blood. I'm the one you would sing the Marine's Hymn to when you would rock me to sleep in my room. I'm your boy. While you were *gone during my teenage years, life became dark for me. Life was no longer beautiful. My Mom was too busy trying to raise my brother and me in addition to putting food on the table, a roof over our heads, and clothes on our backs. When I needed support and guidance with school, you were no longer there for me. I struggled to the point of dropping out. I began to hand around the bad kids around school. I started doing drugs. Mom was so stressed with trying to provide some kind of normal life; she was clueless as to what was happening in my life. And you weren't there to help her or me. Because I was so angry with you and life in general, I became a violent, rebellious, and uncaring person. I was lost and became part of this forsaken world. Where were you? As I entered the most difficult years of a boy's life, you abandoned me when I needed you most. But it made me tough. It hardened me. As I grew older, I convinced myself to accept what had happened as part of life. I had moved on, at least in my mind. Then your new life fell apart and now you had time for me. Now you came back to be a part of my life. But as much as I was happy to have you back, you were a different person. You were no longer someone I could look up to, turn to, or count on to be my father. You were now an alcoholic. I could see that you were no longer a man to be proud of, but a man that I felt pity and embarrassment for. You never recovered. I watched as you slowly but steadily became the child and I was being forced to be the parent. You worked at a fast-food place while I also worked there, making more money. You lost your apartment and started sleeping in your car like a bum. Then you lost your car and truly became a bum, sleeping under the brush and trees by the freeway. Do you know how hard it was for me to see my father live like that? Taking food and blankets to you? U did everything I could to avoid anyone finding out about you or even talking about you. My Mom, with love and sadness, allowed you to come back into the house and stay there as a guest in order for you to get yourself together. But you didn't. You did nothing but live off the kindness and generosity of my Mom. My anger, supplemented by hatred, returned. Do you remember all our fights? They did nothing but kill whatever love I still had for you. I eventually moved out and my Mom decided she had enough as well. Your disability payments had recently kicked in and now I had to find you a place and help you move because you had no car, no license, no friends, and no family other than me to assist you. Since that time, and I must admit partially due to your head trauma from years ago, you were becoming mentally incapable of taking care of yourself, not to mention that it appeared to me that you just didn't care either. Our relationship is something I wish I wouldn't have to live with and I wouldn't wish it on my worst enemy. I truly don't know how I feel about you, about us, anymore. Sometimes, it feels more of an obligation based on pity that I even make an attempt to be a part of your life. Sometimes I think you would end up dead and alone if I wasn't around and I don't need any more emotional damage caused by you. I've had enough for a lifetime. So much, for so long, I've wanted you to be my father again, to have nice and pleasant conversations between father and son. I want to share my life with you, to learn about your life before me, to go out to a ballgame like we used to, to talk like normal adults. But I fear that it will never be. You just don't seem to be capable of it. Even now, after all my pleading and begging with you, you still don't even make an attempt to take care of yourself, to make yourself presentable to others, to learn a hobby, to travel, or basically do anything. For several years now, I've been watching you give up on life and slowly die in front of me and I've been utterly helpless in being able to help you or stop your deterioration and it tears me apart. I have been reaching out to you for 20 years now and I received nothing in return. I would just be happy if you could get your life together and be happy again. Really! That would make all my efforts worthwhile because you're my DAD and I do still love you, even if it's killing me at the same time. I wish I could sit down with you and tell you all of this and more with the sincere hope that you would finally reach out to me, tell me you're sorry, tell me that you never stopped loving your little boy and that you want to be my father again. I have prayed for this and so much more. Even now, with me losing my wife and going through a divorce, I am unable to turn to you for support and advice. Once again, in my time of need, you're not there and a big part of why this is happening to me stems from you absence in my life and how I've dealt with that. You could say that I never quite recovered from what you put me through those many years ago and even now in our current days. But rest assured, although I hold you responsible for many things, I do not blame for my current troubles. I promise! I love you Dad.*

Your Boy!

When this letter was read in my office, even though I was looking at a 30 something year old man, it appeared as though he had stepped back into a time chamber. He sobbed openly while reading the letter and I could tell that he had become that hurt little boy all over again.

When fathers leave, it is erroneous to believe that they are devoid of pain and hurt because of the decision they felt they had to make. It is also important to underscore that men are not always the ones who leave the relationship. However, when women leave their husbands, the majority of these children still end up separated from their fathers.

It was apparent in this letter that both father and son were seriously impacted by their separation. The father was unable to emotionally handle leaving his son, and the son was unable to handle him leaving. Both of them acted out of their pain in negative ways, causing them to hurt the ones they loved the most.

SURROGATE DADS ARE ABSENT TOO

When mothers remarry or involve other father figures in the lives of their children, there is the potential for these surrogate fathers to also abandon sons who are longing for a father figure. Step-father/step-son relationships can be impaired when step-fathers perceive their step-sons to be more closely attached to their mother than they would like. The relationship between a man and his step-son may also suffer because the mother interferes in their relationship. Also, these relationships can be strained when step-fathers come into the home and instantly become the man of the house.

Pre-existing relationships are often difficult to infiltrate, and step-fathers can harbor resentment towards their wives and step-sons when they feel left out or have been offended by their step-sons. Somehow, it seems easier for fathers to forgive the transgressions or perceived transgressions of their biological children than those of their step-children. Unfortunately, these step-sons like all sons are desperately in need of a healthy relationship with a father figure, but rarely do all parties concerned do the necessary work to fix the problem until it is very possibly too late and the relationship is irreparable. When a man does not know how to nor want to fix problems with his step-son, and/or when he has an ax to grind with his wife due to blended family issues, he will emotionally disconnect from both of them.

An example of the impact of the abandonment of a father figure is reflected in another letter written to a step-father who was in the home, yet not quite emotionally available. This gentleman is now in his 70's, and once again, when you read this letter you will get the sense that he is emotionally stuck back in time.

LETTER TO MY DAD – (Unedited)

Dear Dad

Thank you for marrying my mom, for raising us, and for being my dad. Thank you for the many years of providing us with food, clothing, and shelter. Thank you for doing your best to father us, although I know that you never really had a good role model, because while you deeply loved your own father, grandpa only knew how to provide the basics, food, clothing, and shelter. Therefore, you, yourself, did not know how to give of yourself the intangible things, etc. I really needed:

> *Companionship with you*
> *Your involvement in my academic life at school*
> *Your attendance at the father-son sports banquets*
> *Long talks with me about life*
> *Your encouragement of me – a pat on the shoulder*

Oh, how I wish we could have tossed around the football, the baseball, gone fishing or played golf.

Oh how I wish I could have told you about my first kiss. Similarly, I wish you could have discussed with me the facts regarding sex, and other female-male issues.

Oh how I wish you could have coached me in sports. Also, I needed your guidance and pep talk when I was constantly bullied at school. That day when I was severely beaten by two thugs, I wish you could have encouraged me.

Perhaps my development of stuttering was an outward manifestation of my inward turmoil of confusion and low self esteem. That's why in my late teens and early adulthood, I looked for surrogate dads in other men. Even to this day, I still feel incomplete. Yet, and still, I thank you for being my dad.

Your Son!

Some men do not know how to nurture and encourage their sons because of their understanding of what constitutes manhood. A man will devote a great deal of his time to instructing and correcting sons. However, this may explain why males run to their mothers for their emotional connection. This need on the part of sons to be encouraged and nurtured by mothers can sometimes cause men to become angry and they may disconnect from their sons and basically ignore them. Your son needs you to teach him how to be a man, but he also needs a real demonstration of your love and understanding, even if you did not receive it from your father. In fact, you may have to rely on your helper (your wife) to teach you how to minister to the emotional needs of your son.

Based on the information shared in this Chapter, it is apparent that fathers are of vital importance in the lives of boys and men. Also, fathers are important to their daughters in an important way. You can find a discussion about fathers and their role in the lives of daughters in my book, *Keeping it Real! 7 Steps Toward a Healthier You.* If the Saints of God are going to be healthy in their mind, body, and spirit, it is important to discuss and deal with the secret issues to help them to become free.

You too may have lived your life without a father, and you may be broken down inside because of his absence in your life. I just want to remind you of an important Scripture with promise found in 2 Corinthians 6:18:

"I will be a Father to you, and you shall be My sons and daughters says the Lord Almighty."

IT MAY BE TIME TO WRITE A LETTER TO YOUR DAD. FEEL FREE TO BEGIN YOUR LETTER IN THE SPACE PROVIDED BELOW!

Dear Dad....

AFTER WRITING IT, FIND SOMEONE YOU LOVE AND TRUST TO READ YOUR LETTER TO. AFTER YOU FINISH, TEAR IT UP AND BURY IT IN THE DIRT SO YOUR TRUE INNER HEALING CAN BEGIN.

Chapter 6

∞

Shattered Dreams

And we know that all things work together for good to those who love God, to those who are called according to His purpose. Romans 8:28

When I grow up, I am going to be a doctor and help sick people. No when I grow up I am going to have a big restaurant where people can eat their favorite foods. You remember what it was like to have dreams, goals, and aspirations. Most of us can relate to being excited and looking with anticipation to the day when our dreams would come true. But what happens to men when their dreams get shattered and crushed? They cry on the inside, and sometimes act out on the outside.

Most men have dreams and aspirations regarding their life's passion that are fueled by their desire to be a good provider for their family. Unfortunately, many men may suffer because they can't seem to be successful in reaching their goals. Steven agrees that shattered dreams are difficult for men to handle. *"Men cry because of unachieved goals. Some men look around them and their friends are able to buy homes or go where they want to go, but they are unable to get where they want to get in life."*

Disappointment in this area may once again stem from men's perspective on manhood. When one's success as a man is tied to one's achievements in life, it is not surprising that one would suffer emotional pain when one's dreams are short lived.

There are several factors that may contribute to shattered dreams. A dream may become shattered because it is not God's will for it to survive. You can plan all day long, but if your plan does not coincide with God's plan for your life, LOOK OUT, your dream may shatter and fall to the ground. A wise person once said, *"If you really want to make God laugh, tell God your plans."*

Some dreams are shattered because of poor planning and preparation, and inadequate resources. For example, Michael decided to open up his own retail book store. He was very excited about the opportunity to see his dream realized, and without much discussion with his wife, and poor planning, the book store drained all of the family resources, leaving them in a state of bankruptcy. Not only did this business venture wipe them out financially, it negatively impacted the overall quality of their marital relationship.

> *Some dreams are killed by financial constraints, poor timing, and poor planning.*

Dreams can also be shattered into little pieces when men do not receive the support of the women in their lives. It is important to note, however, that men may erroneously believe they are not being supported by their wives because they may confuse women's need to receive information and to be included in the decision making process as disapproval and lack of support.

Ladies, there is no question that we are well within our rights to ask our husbands to discuss every detail of their ideas, including the three B's: BUDGET, BURDENS, and BLESSINGS associated with those ideas.   However, we must be careful in the way we go about requesting the information. Our approach can sometimes feel belittling, disrespectful, and unsupportive to our spouses.

Some of the men I work with admit that many of the mistakes they made in their business dealings probably could have been avoided had they been willing to receive and welcome the insight and wisdom of Godly women.   Unfortunately, some women lack spiritual wisdom and maturity. These women have not learned how to be supportive and helpful to their spouses through prayer and encouragement.

I know about this issue firsthand because I did not always understand how to support the dreams of my husband, [a true visionary leader] because of my own fears of failure and limited faith. He has always had wonderful ideas to make things better for our family, but I grew up observing another wonderful visionary leader in action, my father.   He too had wonderful ideas, but because of limited resources some of his dreams would shatter and fall.

As with any disappointment, it takes its toll on the family and its resources. What I didn't totally understand at the time, my father was a man of faith, just as he is today. You want to know a secret? God would always make a way where there seemed to be no way, and my father was an excellent provider. Well I married a man much like my father, except, he was blessed with more resources. When he began to discuss his ideas, something would churn on the inside of me. I now know it was fear. When we are anxious and fearful, we tend to do whatever we can to control our situation in order to reduce the anxiety. Men, your wives may appear to be controlling, but they are more than likely trying to manage their emotions of fear and anxiety.

Men tend to be more willing to take risks which can be scary for women. Tommy Stewart said, *"You can play it safe, and never realize your dreams, or you can take some risks. That's what makes life interesting."*

It took years for me to accept that my husband was also a man of faith, and it seemed like the moment I acknowledged my fears and buried them, God blessed us even more abundantly. I finally grew up! I became a woman who learned how to support and encourage her husband with joy. I've learned so much about faith through those early experiences.

However, men must allow their women to participate in every aspect of their lives, which is very difficult to do because men have been socialized to carry their own load. That is why so many men have fallen to the ground along with their shattered dreams because the load was too great. Also, women must provide a safe and supportive environment in order for men to open up and share their innermost thoughts and feelings.

DREAM KILLERS

Dreams are sometimes shattered because of male-female relationship issues. Women have to be especially careful in their attempt to support their husbands. Couples have a difficult time in this area because they do not always have the same understanding of the dream, or the female spouse may have experienced some of the consequences of failed attempts in achieving the goal. Further, failure to consult God and wait for an answer will make matters worse.

Males who believe their spouses have killed their dreams start out feeling sad on the inside, but that sadness can quickly turn to anger and bitterness. In this situation, men may fail to talk about what they are really upset about, and when they shut down emotionally, it will not be long before they begin to withhold the love. Since a man needs to be celebrated and respected by his spouse, he tends to function best when she believes in him and is confident that he will do what's best for their family. That is the biggest vote of confidence a man can receive.

When one's dreams have been shattered, one also may feel like a failure. This is especially problematic when men perceive their wives as being more successful in reaching their goals and aspirations in life. Therefore, it is important for women to understand the heartbeat of their men. The provider role is a strong value for many men; so it is important to encourage their efforts, even when the outcome looks scary or even a disaster waiting to happen.

TO MY SISTERS

I know you may have reached the end of your rope. All you need is one more idea, one more dream. I recall saying to my husband, "I wish you would wake up so the dreams will stop coming." My emotions had run rampant, causing me to experience a lot of stress and strain in my life. I had to learn to manage my emotions so I could give my husband all the love, support, and encouragement he desperately needed in order to be successful. I also had to learn to prepare the right environment so my husband could share any and everything with me without fear of entering into World War III.

I decided to pray for my husband every day. I prayed that God would bless him, protect him, and prosper his life. I would even pray for God to enlarge his territory. DON'T GET IT TWISTED! When God prospers your spouse, guess who also reaps the benefits? You and me! I had to change my attitude and increase my faith in order to receive the favor of God.

I know you have convinced yourself that your husband does not care about your feelings. I am encouraging you to avoid holding onto the faulty notion that men do not care about women's feelings when they make bad business decisions causing financial problems for the family. Men do experience feelings of guilt and regret for some of the decisions they have made, After all, your spouse really wants to please you and make you proud of him, and when he fails to do it he silently suffers on the inside. Men just may not communicate those feelings to their spouses. Sisters, you must do whatever you can to let him know that you love and accept him even when he messes up. Remember, you are designed to be his number one cheerleader.

TO MY BROTHERS

You need your wife because she is your helper. I realize you have been taught to go it alone, but that faulty teaching may not be serving you well. God may be showing your wife something you have been too distracted to see. Perhaps you have hurt her by shutting her out and making continual bad decisions because of pride. Apologize to your wife and correct bad habits and behaviors so the quality of your relationship will improve and you can gain the freedom to live your dreams to the fullest.

If your dreams have been shattered, I encourage you to believe God's promise to His children in Romans 8:28: *And we know that all things work together for good to those who love God, to those who are called according to His purpose.* Perhaps your dreams have not been realized because God has something bigger and better in store for you.

I am certain the disciples may have had other plans for their lives. In fact, when Jesus called them they had to give up their plans for the work of the Kingdom. This may be a good time for you to discover what God is really calling you to do to make sure your plans are in line with His plans. When that happens, it will be easy for you to put the pieces of your life back together again.

Chapter 7

∞

Love on the Rocks

Marriage is like a job, and you have to work at it daily. Harold & Henrietta Phillips

The divorce rate among the Body of Christ continues to mirror the divorce rate of the general population.   Marriage can be very challenging and difficult and most couples are unprepared for it for a variety of reasons: (1) Poor role models of marriage to follow, (2) Failure to discuss and agree upon rules, needs, and desires before the wedding, (3) Pre-existing relationships, (4) Financial problems, (5) Poor communication skills, (6) Inability to effectively negotiate cultural differences, and (7) Poor mental, physical, and spiritual health.

These issues can cause couples to fuss and fight constantly leaving one or both of them tired and beat up, and ready to bolt out of the door. When love is on the rocks, both men and women suffer emotionally, just differently. Women are more visibly shaken, and tend to shut down all physical contact. On the other hand men must hide their true feelings, so they tend to disconnect from those they love, and cry silently on the inside.

Men and women also fight differently. Females tend to question, challenge, and/or debate for long periods of time until they feel as though they have either been heard or the issue has been resolved. This approach does not work well for most men who would prefer fewer words to be spoken, and to be left alone until the dust settles. Women also threaten to leave with no intention of doing so. They are simply trying to garner a response from their clueless husband.

> *When it comes down to the relationship with a man's wife or girlfriend, I think something within that relationship will make a man cry, and he will cry either internally or outwardly. Vernon*

Many couples have not learned how to utilize the concept of *Emotional Intelligence*, which is the process by which to gauge the emotional temperature of yourself and others before speaking and behaving, to avoid acting out in inappropriate and destructive ways. *Emotional Intelligence* is a guide to help you to respond at the appropriate time and manner to minimize miscommunication, misunderstandings, and even blow-ups that have the potential to lead to mental, emotional, and/or physical abuse.

For the women reading this book, you may erroneously believe that your spouse or mate does not care about you anymore because he appears to be disconnected from you. That may not be the case! Rather, males tend to respond and react to women the way they have been socialized to respond and react. It is important for you to know that men have the need to fix problems. When men believe they are unsuccessful in solving problems they tend to retreat because of the faulty belief they have failed in serving a useful purpose in the relationship.

Women may have a difficult time when men retreat so they attempt to pull them back into the discussion [fight] that they are ill-prepared to engage in at the time by any means necessary. If you are guilty of this strategy, ladies, you are NOT exercising the concept of Emotional Intelligence that I alluded to earlier.

I NEED TO FIX IT

We have discovered many of the factors that make marriage difficult resulting in silent tears for men. As stated earlier, some men struggle in their relationships because they are unable to fix the problems. Males have been socialized to be very logical, so they tend to go into FIX IT mode when their spouse shares a concern with them.

Sometimes men become the self appointed savior of the family, and when they are not given the opportunity to fix problems they feel worthless. This FIX-IT mentality can be problematic for some women because they don't always want their men to fix the problem. More often than not, women just want their men to listen and be supportive. However ladies, you will not be able to discuss things with your spouse in the same way you discuss things with your girlfriends. WE USE TOO MANY WORDS!

Rob, a participant of this project admitted that he sometimes gets very frustrated when his wife cries or is upset. *"I sometimes look down and say, what are you crying for? What is the problem? Then as a STRONG man would, I just want to fix it. The reason for my frustration is, I cannot always FIX IT."*

> *I am always thinking about how to fix what's wrong or hurting her. There has got to be a way to FIX IT. Leonard*

I remember coming home after a stressful day at the office. It seemed like at least four of my clients that day decided to express thoughts of harming themselves, resulting in a very challenging day for me. While I could not share the specifics with my beloved, I did share that I was frustrated and tired of the work, which was a normal reaction to the type of day I had.

Before I could complete my sentence, my husband looked me in my eyes and emphatically said these words: JUST QUIT! I could not believe my ears. I thought to myself, he has gone mad. How can I quit? I love what I do. I was hoping he would have taken me in his arms and comforted me, gone upstairs and ran me a hot bubble bath, made me a nice cup of tea, and given me the opportunity to continue sharing my frustrations with him.

Instead my husband responded in the way some men respond to problems: **I NEED TO FIX IT**! When I appeared disappointed by his quick solution to my problem, he was hurt and disappointed. I wanted him to understand what Tommy S. one of the participants of this project so appropriately and accurately explained: *"Women do not always need Superman, sometimes they need Clark Kent."* Superman represents the super hero who comes to save the day, while Clark Kent represents the ordinary man who is there on a daily basis to attend to the everyday needs of the woman of his dreams. Superman gets the job done and moves on to the next challenge, wherever that may be.

I JUST CAN'T PLEASE HER

When men think they have disappointed their spouses, they begin to doubt their ability to please them. Men may suffer on the inside when they believe they have failed in pleasing those they love. For example, Ralph was feeling very defeated in his marriage of 21 years because he believed he had been unsuccessful in pleasing his wife, Joy. Joy had recently reminded Ralph that their house was in serious need of repairs. After the third time of reminding him, Ralph became very agitated and irritable. He shot back, "I know what the house needs. If you were doing more to help, everything would get done."

At first glance it appeared that Ralph was angry because Joy was not helping enough. WRONG! Ralph was really feeling like a failure because he had obviously disappointed his wife. He did not believe she appreciated all the other things he was doing, which was not the case at all. She was merely reminding him of things that needed to be done to prevent the cost from accelerating later.

Ralph's thoughts, although irrational were present because of his understanding of what constitutes manhood. Remember, a man is supposed to provide, fix problems, protect, and take care of the needs of the family. When he believes he is failing at his job for whatever reason, he cries on the inside which sometimes makes him explode on the outside. Sometimes men give up on the marriage because of the belief, although irrational at times, that they are unable to please their wives.

Further, men sometimes feel undervalued, unappreciated, and disrespected by the women they love. Whether real or imagined, these thoughts and feelings can lead to emotional cut-off and in extreme cases men may seek comfort and even revenge in the arms of another woman.

Men may also have some difficulty in meeting the emotional needs of women because of what they observed in their family of origin. For example, men who did not see an outward expression of love and affection by their parents while growing up may have a difficult time being affectionate with their wives. Similarly, men who did not see their fathers bring gifts home for mothers on special days (i.e., Valentine's Day, anniversary, birthday) and non-special days may also find it difficult to adopt that practice.

When wives complain about the lack of affection from their men, they typically respond by laying out their stellar record of buying the house, car, and other benefits as a demonstration of their love. This impressive yet faulty explanation by men is usually not acceptable to women who feel love deprived. Therefore, women may continue to complain to men about their need for love and affection, making men believe: I JUST CAN'T PLEASE HER!

DON'T TELL ME WHAT TO DO

Men may also secretly harbor anger and resentment when they believe their wives are treating them like a child. This thinking can sometimes occur because of baggage from the past. Men may have negative messages buried in their suitcase from mothers, caregivers, siblings, and/or past relationships that continue to haunt them. For example, men that have been raised primarily by women may have a hard time receiving instructions from a woman, even if she is his wife. Wives usually have no idea why their husband is acting out. A woman will say, "I just asked him to take out the trash and he flipped out." He is simply responding to the feedback he received from those early women in his life.

I was listening intently to a woman who told me her husband would become very irritated with her when she asked him to do anything around the house. It did not matter if she asked him nicely or otherwise, the response was still the same. This perplexed woman became very frustrated because she did not know what she was doing wrong to cause him to respond so negatively to her requests.

When I asked her husband what his early experiences were like in his home, he shared that he grew up in a single female headed household, and as the oldest child, he felt like the slave of the house. He stated, *"My mother barked orders at me all day long, from taking the trash out to getting a glass of cold water from the refrigerator, just when my favorite part of the movie was on."*

This young man did not make the connection until I began to probe him about his early experiences. As it turned out, every time the frustrated wife would ask her husband to assist her, he responded to her in the way he wanted to respond to his mother, but could not. You see, the tape recorded version of his mother's instructions was tucked away neatly in his suitcase, preventing him from responding to his wife appropriately. Instead, he was secretly telling his wife, **DON'T TELL ME WHAT TO DO!**

In this case, it is very important for men to dump out those things in their suitcase that may cause them to harbor resentment and anger towards an unintended victim, who usually happens to be the person closest to them.

Because of the complexities surrounding marriage, men sometimes experience loneliness because they are disconnected from their rib. Many men look to their wives for friendship and companionship. When problems in the relationship due to misunderstandings and mistakes occur, it is a lonely place for men to be. It is also lonely for women, but that is a subject that will be covered in another book.

God designed the institution of marriage so that both men and women could have companionship. However, failure to follow God's plan for marriage will ultimately result in suffering and pain; not only for the men who are the focus of this book, but the women and children they love.

Chapter 8

∞

Since I Lost My Babies

And be kind to one another, tenderhearted, forgiving one another, even as God in Christ forgave you. Ephesians 4:32

The loss of children due to family disruption was a serious source of inner turmoil and emotional upheaval for some of the participants of this project. Men in our society have received a bad reputation because they are believed to abandon their children and fail to support them financially. Unfortunately, some men are guilty as charged with no good explanation for their behavior. They fit the "deadbeat dad" profile.

When men fail to support their children financially it affects their socioeconomic status and overall well-being, especially for children being raised in single female headed households. This lack of support can far too often contribute to a generational curse of poverty. It is important to underscore here, that people who live in impoverished conditions are highly at risk of experiencing mental and physical health challenges because of the health disparities that exist for the poor.

Contrary to the aforementioned reality, there are good men who are also separated from their children against their will, which causes them to cry silent tears. The primary reasons good men are separated from their children are: 1) A bad divorce; 2) Military assignments or relocation; (3) Poor relationship with the mother of their children; and 4) Death of a child.

According to Steven, a participant of this project:

So many people have gone through divorce and separation, and some men have great challenges in staying connected to their kids. I am speaking of men who want to be connected. Some of the men I know have had tremendous challenges with their ex-spouses and that's been a tough place for men to be. When men are disconnected from their children they cry real tears.

Rob explained that the loss of his children due to death and divorce had a profound impact on his life:

I have cried personally over the loss of my kids. I lost two boys at young ages. They both died. Then after the break-up of my first marriage, I lost my girls. I have two daughters. That has been the most devastating thing in my life."

A young man came to see me whose separation from his children not only caused him to cry, but contributed to him suffering from a depressive disorder. Matt came to my office very reluctantly. His wife Pam had given him a serious ultimatum: Counseling or Divorce. Pam wanted me to evaluate Matt for depression because of some of the symptoms he presented with at home. Matt was indifferent more days than not. After work he retreated to his room, and when he did eat, he ate in his room away from the family. Pam reported that Matt was very irritable and snappy, and one day he came close to hitting her.

Initially Matt was very guarded when undergoing the assessment process, which can be very daunting at best. But it wasn't long before Matt leaned back on the couch and began to tell a story that is becoming more and more common; and often the source of men's emotional pain.

I asked Matt to tell me about his prior experiences so I could get a better historical picture to assist me in making a more accurate assessment. He told me about his early experiences as the middle son of five siblings. He described his childhood as good for the first 12 years of his life; but his world was shattered on his 13th birthday when his father came home after work, called all the children into the living room, and told them he was leaving. Matt recalled hearing his mother sobbing in the bedroom and just as quickly as his father lowered the boom, he picked up the suitcase that was tied together with an old belt and waiting at the door, and he left.

Matt described himself as "numb" as he heard the front door slam shut. The next thing he knew, he was placed in a position of trying to prevent his younger 10 year old sister from bolting out the front door after her father. Matt could still hear his little sister screaming and crying for their father to come back, a visual memory that is not easy for Matt to erase to this day.

He explained that his father rarely came to pick them up because of his relationship with their mother. When he did, the children of his new girlfriend were waiting eagerly in the car. Matt remembered being very angry and resentful because his dad seemed to spend more time with his girlfriend's children than he did his own. Further, the presence of these other innocent children caused his mother to become even sadder and more distant.

Matt stated his mother was good to them, but she was not emotionally present because of her sadness about the break-up of her marriage and her ex-husband's sudden and unannounced remarriage. In fact, Matt said his mother was angry, bitter, and sad until the day she died, which was a few years earlier than our session in my office. He now believes his mother was suffering from depression, which may have contributed to Matt's development of the disease. It is common when a parent suffers from depression [a treatable disease] that one or more of the children will also be diagnosed with the disease because of a genetic predisposition or environmental factors.

Matt had a difficult time in school because of his emotional scars, and found himself in trouble academically during his adolescent years. Although he was very angry on the inside, rather than Matt acting out violently like some young men do who are harboring anger and resentment, he simply shut down. This resulted in poor academic success throughout his middle school and most of his high school years. He was not a problem for his teachers. He just didn't do any work.

Miraculously, Matt seemed to be able to pull it together, graduated high school and enrolled in the local community college. After completing his continuing education courses, Matt transferred to the university where he met the girl of his dreams who later became his wife and the mother of his three children.

Matt married Rosalyn as soon as they graduated college, and shortly thereafter the children began to arrive quickly. It did not take too long for this young couple who had never observed healthy models of marriage to begin to have problems of their own. Matt explained that their biggest challenges had to do with poor communication skills and finances.

Another factor that contributed to their problems was their inability to adequately bond together as a couple because of their new role as parents. Please know that this factor is not always a source of concern for couples. However, it can be a source of contention if one of the spouses is unhappy when the children come. Matt felt betrayed because his young bride refused to comply with their agreement to delay having children. So after 5 years of marriage, and three young children later (ages 2, 3, and 4), the promising couple became divorced.

The day Matt's father walked out on them, he promised himself that he would never walk out on his kids. This promise was ever present on Matt's mind. He admitted, however, that both he and his wife were very immature and allowed their anger and hurt towards one another to impact the way they engaged in their fight over the children.

Therefore, the two of them fought bitterly over custody of the children. Even though Rosalyn was granted full custody and Matt received weekly visitation rights, nobody won. Finally, Matt became so frustrated about the never ending battles with his ex and the children's reluctance to visit him because of loyalty to their mother, until he stopped trying to visit the children.

Matt recalled going to the bank each month to get a money order so he could send the child support payments faithfully. He was determined to not repeat the patterns of his father, since he seemed to never pay child support consistently. It wasn't long before Matt left the area and moved to another city, where he met and married Pam his second wife.

After five years of marriage, Matt and Pam had their first and only child together, a son who was now 12 years old. Sadly, Matt had not seen his other three children for a long time. His ex-wife remarried and told him in a telephone conversation before he left the city that he need not worry about the children anymore because they had a new father who loved them and would take care of them.

Matt reported throwing himself into his new marriage and family; but primarily his work. However, he never got over being separated from his first set of children. Further, Matt's 12 year old son was beginning to ask to meet his three older siblings which was another source of pain for Matt. This is a problem for some adults who never had a chance to meet their half-siblings because of family drama. They find themselves on a never ending search to find lost relatives. Unfortunately, when they do locate their family, real relationships may be difficult to build.

After my assessment with Matt, it was clear that he was suffering from a depressive disorder which probably started when he was 13 years old but grew worse after losing his first three children. Matt was crying silent tears because he lost his babies.

In our society today many people, especially women are very critical towards men who do not fight to remain connected to their children. Men may give up on being with their children because they cannot emotionally handle the constant fighting and bickering that women are sometimes better at. This does not excuse men from seeking legal assistance to help them to receive and maintain their parental rights.

It is not uncommon for hurting mothers who refuse to forgive their ex-husbands to make it difficult for men to be involved in their children's lives. Therefore, I want to encourage my sisters to avoid verbally assaulting your ex in the presence of your children. That behavior can cause more harm than good and it may impact your children for the rest of their lives. Make the commitment to love your children more than you dislike their father. Scripture teaches, *Vengeance is mine, I will repay says the Lord. Romans 12:19*

In addition, some men who are the custodial parent of their children, can be just as guilty of verbally attacking the character of their ex-wife in front of the children. In both cases, children are forced to choose between two parents, resulting in a NO-WIN situation for all concerned. So to you my brothers, I would like to extend the same encouragement. Allow God to fight your battles, so that you can be a good witness before God and your children.

Of course, the ideal situation is for people to commit to do the necessary work to preserve their marriage and family at all cost. But let's keep it real! This commitment will require a much higher level of Spiritual maturity on each person's part in the relationship. For some reason, the Saints of God are moving toward the front of the line in terms of bailing out of marriages that are in need of repair. While I am not sanctioning divorce, I am recommending that whatever decision you make, find a way to place your children's interest over your personal interests so that the impact of your decision will be less traumatic for them.

It's been tough being separated from my daughter who lives in another state. It's my joy to call and speak to her. It picks up my spirits. Sometimes we play phone tag, and maybe 2 or 3 days later, I get to talk to her. I'm so happy because I am always concerned that something may have happened to her. Stan

Men sometimes walk away because they cannot handle the pressures at home. In this day where some men do not make adequate income to provide for a family, they will walk away because they believe themselves to be a failure. To complicate matters, these same men will find themselves another family which can be more devastating to the family they left behind. I heard a pastor tell this story which helped me to understand this issue from another perspective.

There was a man who was having a difficult time in his marital relationship. His wife complained that he was NOT helping the family enough financially. He had been laid off his job, and even though he was looking for work, he was unable to find anything. His wife worked, and she continued to beat him down each day because she was going out to work and he was staying at home.

Finally, the man felt like he was a total failure in his home, so he left his wife and 2 children. It wasn't long before he united with another woman who had 6 children. I know you are wondering how he could leave his wife and two children that he was having difficulty providing for, to move in with a woman with six children to care for? I had the same question in my mind.

The pastor explained that the woman with 6 children had never had much help from her children's father. So even if this new man could only buy one loaf of bread, it was more than she had ever received on a consistent basis. She was grateful for it and this new man became her hero. Men need to be the hero, and when they believe they can no longer hold that title, they may start looking for other places where the title can be respected. While this response is certainly not one I endorse, it is a reality nonetheless.

Some fathers are separated from their children because of military assignments or work opportunities. I am sure you remember hearing some of the elders talk about men in their communities who left home to find work and some of them never returned. People demonized those men, but when taking into consideration the mental make-up of men, it is not surprising that men would not return, especially if they were unable to find a better way of life for their families. Remember, men have been socialized to believe that a REAL MAN provides for his family. If he is unable to provide, he perceives himself to be less than a man.

Berkeley, a participant of this project shared his experiences of what it was like to be forced to leave his family in order to provide for them:

> *I remember having to leave Barbados to seek employment and education abroad. That was a very gut-wrenching thing that I had to do because I had to leave my family, initially to go to Canada to set up our future life there. My kids were very young at the time and when I arrived there, I did not get a job immediately to provide for them the way I imagined I would be able to. Significantly too, was the fact that the educational system there did not recognize any of my degrees from Barbados. So I had to start from the beginning, working a part-time job and finally two full-time jobs in order to make it. I brought a lot of grief with me because of my situation, and my desire was to become stable enough to bring my family to Canada.*

Lastly, when a man loses his baby because of death, he experiences a terrible loss. It is interesting to note here, that fathers may respond and react to the death of a child differently than do mothers. However, men are hurt and devastated by the death of a child, even though they tend to grieve differently. Women sometimes believe that their husbands are not taking the death as hard as they are which causes them to minimize the impact of the loss on men. They have not been given permission to break down and deal with their problems emotionally. Rather, they have been taught to deal with problems intellectually.

Differences between men and women make it difficult for men to grasp an understanding of how to help women when they are responding emotionally to problems. When a man loses a child he feels helpless. Further, it may be even more difficult for him to cope with the loss if he feels like he has failed his wife once again. He is not only dealing with his own grief and sadness over the death of his child, he is also dealing with the fact that he cannot fix this problem for his wife.

In Mark 5:22-43, Jairus the synagogue ruler sought Jesus to heal his 12 year old daughter. By the time Jesus arrived to their home, the young girl was dead. I can only imagine that Jairus was not only devastated because his daughter was dead, but he had to look into the eyes of his wife and acknowledge defeat. After all he was unable to fix the problem, even after seeking and finding the Master healer everyone had been raving about.

When Jesus arrived to the home, everyone was weeping, but Jairus was the voice of reason. He said in the 35th verse, "My daughter is dead: why are you bothering the Master any further? In other words, it is what it is, so let's move on; words spoken by a true man. Jesus understood that beneath the surface Jairus was experiencing feelings of fear and he lacked faith. It was possible that Jairus had to conceal his true condition because of manhood, while his wife allowed her feelings to be known.

Losing a child for any reason is devastating for both parents. However, men's inability to grieve in the same way women do sometimes causes them to break down internally, or to become overly involved in work or other activities. In these cases, it is much easier for men to DO than to BE! Failure to understand these differences can negatively impact both men and women's healing process.

WRITE A LOVE NOTE TO YOUR WIFE!

WRITE A LOVE NOTE TO YOUR CHILDREN!

Chapter 9

∞

Social Injustice

I have a dream that one day ….. Martin Luther King, Jr.

The participants of this project overwhelmingly cited social injustice as a significant factor in the status of men's emotional health. The social injustices in society increase the likelihood of men, especially men of color, being denied those things that are beneficial for them to adequately provide for and protect their families. There are a number of social injustices that are important to this discussion. However, we will focus our attention on the impact of racism, the criminal justice system, and socioeconomics on men's emotional well-being and ultimately the well-being of their family.

WHAT'S RACE GOT TO DO WITH IT?

Although we live in a modern society in the 21st Century, people of color experience racism on a daily basis. These encounters may be even more pronounced for men who may experience more overt forms of racism. Yes, racism is alive and well, and it rears its ugly head in a variety of destructive ways.

Contemporary racism is much like the AIDS virus. It keeps changing forms, making it very difficult to treat.

Men of color all over the world have few if any outlets to discuss their true feelings about their experiences of racism and discrimination. When they do, they are reminded of how far they have come and all the accomplishments that have been made since the Civil Rights Movement. However, that does not seem to erase the burden men of color bear because of the potential for them to be a victim of some form of racism.

We are witnessing one of the most fascinating elections of all time, with the first Black man, Senator Barack Obama in the lead of a tight democratic race for the presidential nomination. It is pretty clear that Senator Obama has not been exempt from everyday acts of racism. He is a bright and intelligent man who I believe understands better than anyone the true racial climate in America. He has simply chosen to do what many men of color are forced to do on a daily basis, **KEEP ON PUSHING!** It is obvious that Senator Obama is optimistic about America's potential to unite as a diverse nation, with the full capability of promoting and ensuring liberty and justice for all. But not all men of color are as optimistic.

Racism affects everyone in negative ways, and it can serve as another factor that makes men cry secret tears. According to Vernon, a participant of this project, *"racism will make you cry."* Some men are forced to secretly deal with their pain in order to prevent their families from experiencing excessive fear and worry about their well-being.

Men of color, especially Black and Brown men are still victims of Racial Profiling, which refers to the practice of police targeting them for traffic stops because of the belief that these males are more likely to be engaged in criminal activity. These men are constantly on guard to protect themselves from this type of social injustice. In their attempt to cope with this racist practice, men of color routinely develop "Healthy Cultural Paranoia" which is a healthy strategy used to help Black and Brown men to prepare themselves to avoid places and situations that make them vulnerable to being targeted and harassed.

For example, my husband refuses to drive through certain communities in Southern California because of their reputation for high incidents of racially profiling Black motorists. Not only do these incidents create emotional distress because of the men's personal experience with law enforcement, there is also concern about the potential for their sons and other male family members and friends to experience the same type of treatment or worse.

Racism affects the quality of one's life (Harrell, 2000); and it can contribute to poor mental health. According to Harrell, racism can lead to anxiety, depression, hostility, and trauma-related symptoms. People of color can also become paranoid because of real experiences of past racism, which can make one suspicious of everyone who is different and cause psychological impairment. Harrell further suggests that racism can contribute to the development of diseases such as, hypertension and cardiovascular reactivity.

Racism can also impact one's ability to connect socially with those who are ethnically different which may negatively affect intra and intergroup relations and job performance. Harrell stated that racism can also impact one's faith in God.

According to a CBS News report on May 26, 2008:

"Racism is an underlying factor in why Black men in the United States have an overall death rate which is almost 50% higher than that of White men."

In a recent research report aired on CBS News on May 26, 2008, it was found that "Racism Kills."

The report further reveals that racism may be the missing variable in research on black-white differences in health. "While socio-economic status was the major contributor to the disparity in death rate, racism is believed to underpin differences in medical care and health-related behavior, as well as to influence opportunities to maintain and improve health."

Rob a participant of this project shared his reaction to racism in America:

Some of the challenges Black men have had are horrific. Unlike some of our counterparts, as Black men, we have had to deal with life very differently. We had to strive so much harder to gain recognition as an intelligent functional man. So you work so hard until it makes you cry. You say to yourself, why do I have to go through all this just to get you to understand that I am just like you? It is tough for a Black man in America. I've seen it all in my lifetime. Basically, Black men and women should be insane because of what we have had to endure.

Racism is not a new concept. You may remember in the 12th Chapter of Numbers, Miriam and Aaron, Moses' siblings criticized Moses because he married an Ethiopian woman. Some in the Christian community argue that they simply criticized Moses because they were jealous of his power. However, I wonder if they would have criticized Moses' mate selection had his wife shared his same ethnicity? Their actions were very troubling to mild mannered Moses, who was probably silently suffering on the inside because of their racist behavior.

Another social injustice that is in part racially motivated is the high number of men of color who are in the penal system. According to a report published by Gayle Ford, "the proportion of jail imprisonment of Blacks is five times higher than the rate of Whites." These statistics concluded that there are more Black men in prison than in college. Further, 44% of state and federal prisoners in 2003 were Black compared to 35% White, 19% Latino, and 2% other ethnicities.

These statistics are startling, and while many young men may have committed crimes and are incarcerated justifiably, social injustice as it relates to poverty, homelessness, joblessness, and racism may be contributing to these troubling statistics.

Tommy S., one of the participants of this project said: *"Men do cry, but they cry in secret. They get locked up and end up doing 25 to life. Men cry in prison. They are crying for help. We need to stop this epidemic NOW!*

Men are also crying because they cannot adequately take care of their families financially. We are in the midst of a recession and according to the recent statistics, the impact of the current economic context on Black men and boys is stark. For example, in New York City, 49% of all Black men are unemployed. These statistics will certainly make one cry. Poverty is a concern for men of all ethnic backgrounds, however.

Donnie, a participant of this project shared his concerns about the economic plight of the family:

Men cry when they are unable to support their family the way they want. Being physically disabled, it's hard to see your family want something and you're not able to give it to them. You want to work, but you cannot. You don't want to turn to robbing and stealing, so you just have to deal with it within yourself.

In summary, this Chapter has presented some of the issues men, especially Black men face. Failure to address these issues in a proactive and responsible way will continue to impact men and their families in negative and perhaps destructive ways. Men without a strong and secure relationship with God may be even more vulnerable to breaking down emotionally when they experience injustices of any kind. Remember, God is a Shield for you, your Glory, and the lifter of your head. Psalms 3:3

PLEASE RESPOND TO THE FOLLOWING QUESTIONS:

1. WHAT ARE SOME OF THE SOCIAL INJUSTICES YOU HAVE PERSONALLY EXPERIENCED?

2. HOW DID THOSE EXPERIENCES IMPACT YOUR LIFE?

3. HOW DID YOU COPE WITH THE PAIN?

PERSONAL REFLECTIONS

PART III

∞

CONSEQUENCES OF MEN'S SILENT PAIN

Chapter 10

∞

Psychological Damage

And be renewed in the spirit of your mind... Ephesians 4:23

We have discussed some of the critical issues that make men cry, and now in this section of this book we turn our attention to some of the consequences of their silent pain. Throughout this book the point has been well taken that men do not have the same emotional outlet for expressing themselves, making them more at-risk for experiencing psychological damage. In this Chapter, we will explore the different types of psychological damage that affects men when they suffer from unacknowledged and untreated emotional pain and distress.

I'M NOT CRAZY!

According to the most recent report of the National Institute of Mental Health, men suffer from one or more of the following major psychological disorders: Depressive Disorders, Anxiety Disorders, or Substance Abuse Disorders. Unfortunately, some men, especially within the African American community, fail to acknowledge their condition and receive appropriate help for their condition.

Men who exhibit some of the signs and symptoms of depression and anxiety, such as irritability and hostility, paranoid thinking and worry, may find other ways to explain their symptoms. For example, I will often hear men describe their condition in the following ways: "I am having a bad day," or "I am just tired." Failure to acknowledge their condition is problematic making them more at risk of acting out in destructive ways.

COMMON SYMPTOMS OF DEPRESSION IN MALES

- Anger and frustration
- Violent behavior
- Serious risks are taken, such as reckless driving and extramarital sex
- Avoidance of family, friends, and pleasurable activities
- Complaints of fatigue
- Loss of interest in work, hobbies, and sex

There are a variety of reasons Black men fail to seek help for emotional/psychological issues:

(1) They may avoid seeking help because of the stigma and negative stereotypes associated with mental illness. Persons in need of mental health services in the Black community are often viewed as "crazy." This stereotype may make it more difficult for Black males to seek help for their emotional/mental health needs.

Further, it may be difficult for men to seek help from institutions that have traditionally been oppressive.

(2) Black men tend to view emotional problems as a sign of weakness. Seeking professional help may suggest that they are unable to rely on themselves for handling problems and situations which may be a threat to their manhood.

(3) Some men without adequate financial resources and insurance benefits may be unable to afford these services.

(4) Mental health services are not always available by mental health professionals who understand the unique cultural perspective and issues related to Black males in the United States.

(5) Men of all ethnicities may avoid seeking help because of the belief that seeking help for mental health issues is a sign that their faith is weak and/or a reflection of sin in their lives.

DEPRESSION

Clinical vs. Situational

- Clinical Depression
    o Severe depression that interferes with one's daily functioning. There must be impairment in one of the following: work, home, school.
    o Often referred to as a chemical imbalance in the brain and is best treated by a combination of medication and psychotherapy
- Situational Depression
    o The type of depression we all experience from time to time due to situations and life circumstances. However, untreated or unacknowledged situational depression can result in clinical depression.

SYMPTOMS OF DEPRESSION –
National Institute of Mental Health

- Persistent sad, anxious, or "empty" mood
- Feelings of hopelessness, pessimism
- Feelings of guilt, worthlessness, helplessness
- Loss of interest or pleasure in hobbies and activities that were enjoyed, including sex
- Decreased energy, fatigue, being "slowed down"
- Difficulty concentrating, remembering, making decisions
- Insomnia, early-morning awakening, or oversleeping
- Appetite and/or weight loss or overeating and weight gain
- Thoughts of death or suicide, suicide attempts
- Restlessness, irritability

- Persistent physical symptoms that do not respond to treatment, such as headaches, digestive disorders, and chronic pain
- Abnormal or excessive elation
- Unusual irritability
- Decreased need for sleep
- Grandiose notions
- Increased talking
- Racing thoughts
- Inappropriate social behavior

WARNING SIGNS OF SUICIDE

- The individual is talking or joking about suicide (e.g., committing suicide themselves or talking about it in general)
- The individual is preoccupied with death and dying (e.g., recurring death themes in music, literature, drawings, writing letters or leaving notes referring to death or "the end)
- The individual is making statements about reuniting with a deceased loved one.
- The individual has trouble eating and sleeping
- The individual experiences drastic changes in their behavior
- The individual withdraws and isolates from family, friends, or social activities
- The individual loses interest in things they care about (e.g., hobbies, work, school)
- The individual gives away personal possessions
- The individual is making statements about hopelessness, helplessness, or worthlessness (e.g., life is useless. Everyone would be better off without me. It doesn't matter. I won't be around much longer anyway. I wish I could just disappear.

SUICIDE RISK FACTORS

- The individual has attempted suicide before
- A family member has successfully committed suicide
- The individual takes unnecessary risks that might be life threatening or dangerous
- The individual has had a recent severe loss or losses
- The individual loses interest in their personal appearance
- The individual increases alcohol and/or drug use
- The individual is a young Black male, especially between the ages of 10-14

SYMPTOMS OF ANXIETY

- Excessive anxiety and worry
- Restlessness or feeling keyed up or on edge
- Easily fatigued
- Difficulty concentrating or mind going blank
- Irritability
- Muscle tension
- Sleep disturbance
- Other classifications or anxiety disorders
    - Panic attacks
    - Obsessive compulsive disorders
    - Post traumatic stress disorders
    - Acute stress disorders
    - Adjustment disorders

SUBSTANCE ABUSE DISORDERS

- Recurrent substance use resulting in a failure to fulfill major role obligations at work, school or home (e.g., repeated absences or poor work performance related to substance use, substance-related absences, suspensions, neglect of children or household
- Recurrent substance use in situations in which it is physically hazardous (e.g., driving an automobile or operating a machine when impaired by substance use
- Recurrent substance-related legal problems (e.g., arrests for substance related disorderly conduct)
- Continued substance use despite having persistent or recurrent social or interpersonal problems caused or exacerbated by the effects of the substance (e.g., arguments with spouse or partner about consequences of intoxication, physical fights)

Failure to receive appropriate treatment for any of the disorders mentioned above can have a serious impact on men and the people who love them. Further, when men are not psychologically/emotionally healthy, they tend to engage in the self-destructive behaviors that were mentioned earlier in this book, in their attempt to cope with their pain. Men sometimes use drugs, alcohol, affairs, pornography, excessive shopping, eating, and gambling as forms of self-medication. Unfortunately, each of these strategies can lead to destructive and sometimes deadly outcomes.

In addition, failure to appropriately treat psychological disorders, more specifically depressive disorders, makes men more vulnerable for engaging in violent behaviors. There is growing awareness that perpetrators of domestic violence may be suffering from some form of untreated depressive disorder. Therefore, it is imperative for men, especially those who are secretly suffering on the inside to become more comfortable with getting a mental health check-up to ensure good mental health.

WHAT KIND OF PSYCHOLOGICAL/EMOTIONAL DAMAGE HAVE YOU EXPERIENCED BECAUSE OF SILENT TEARS?

Chapter 11

∞

Physical Damage

Or do you not know that your body is the temple of the Holy Spirit who is in you, whom you have from God, and you are not your own? I Corinthians 6:19

Those who continue to silently suffer from emotional distress are also at risk of experiencing a variety of physical health challenges, such as heart disease, hypertension, diabetes, cancers, and HIV-AIDS. Death rates for African American males are at least twice that of African American females for most of the 5 leading causes of death.

African American men have higher death rates than any other population. Lung cancer is the leading cause of cancer death among all African Americans, but over twice as many African American males than females die from lung cancer. Prostate cancer is the second leading cause of cancer death among African American males. One out of every four males who dies from HIV infections is African American.

Excessive stress can also affect men's psychological and physical health. The three most common forms of stress among males is job related stress, financial stress, and relationship stress.

Men who are secretly suffering from inner pain and turmoil may be much more at-risk of experiencing high levels of stress, which can then result in overall poor health.

Men can also experience emotional pain and suffering when their physical health is not good. Donnie, one of the participants of this project shared his thoughts and feelings about the impact of his physical health condition on the quality of his life:

> *Some men are strong and work all their lives, and never get sick. But at a young age I was sick and fell from a two-story building and that just stopped my physical ability to work or hold down a job or anything like that. I have diabetes and it affects me badly sometimes, and it keeps me from working. It's hard because I want to work but I can't.*

Unfortunately, men may experience symptoms of physical distress and fail to seek medical attention in a timely manner, making their condition worse. Wives spend a great deal of their time trying to encourage their spouses to go to the doctor. However, because of some of the factors we discussed in previous chapters in this book, men's resentment towards their wives telling them what to do, or their need to fix problems themselves may contribute to their failure to seek help when necessary.

Chapter 12

∞

Spiritual Damage

For if you live according to the flesh you will die; but if by the Spirit you put to death the deeds of the body, you will live. Romans 8:13

The most important consequence of silent suffering may be the spiritual damage that occurs when one is suffering emotionally. Spiritual damage refers to impairment in one's spiritual life making one experience a disconnection from God. Men who are unhealthy tend to have a difficult time remaining in true fellowship with God and the people of God.

Perhaps this movement away from God is caused by men's participation in destructive and unhealthy behaviors that are in direct opposition to the Word of God. When people choose destructive and unhealthy coping strategies, that is a sign of Spiritual immaturity which results from one's consistent walking in the flesh as opposed to walking in the Spirit.

Further, men who are too spiritually damaged may be unable to live out their purpose and continue the mission of Christ. Sadly, spiritually damaged men may miss out on some of the blessings of the Lord because of their condition. When one is not following the call of Christ through obedience to His will and His way it is difficult for one to experience true inner peace and joy.

However, it is important to note that although men may continue their participation in religious practices this does not mean they are spiritually connected to God. Some men who are spiritually damaged continue to attend regular church services, and they may even be involved in ministry. However, they may not be living a Godly lifestyle.

It is also very difficult to exercise the Spiritual disciplines of prayer, fasting, praise, and worship when one is emotionally and physically bankrupt. Spiritually damaged men may be very critical of others, including the church which can make it hard for them to make an investment into the Kingdom by sowing their time, talent, and treasury into the ministry.

Another reason silent suffering men may become spiritually damaged is their unwillingness to forgive spouses and others who have hurt them. Since it is hard for some men to acknowledge feelings of anger, sadness, and unforgiveness, it may take them a longer time to heal from their open wounds. When men are suffering from emotional pain, they tend to be too wounded for service to their families, their communities, and to God.

> Harboring unforgiveness and bitterness is like drinking poison expecting the other person to die.

A ROYAL INVITATION

There is an interesting story found in the 9th chapter of 2 Samuel where David invited Mephibosheth, the son of Jonathan to live at the palace as one of his sons because of the kindness Jonathan showed him years earlier. Mephibosheth was born into royalty and lived in the palace until a war broke out and his nurse maid heard that it was getting close, and in her haste to flee, she dropped Mephibosheth, causing him to become disabled. His physical impairment and the demise of his father and grandfather Saul caused him to be moved to Lo Debar, a place where others with disabilities lived.

Now after all these years, David is King and he is calling for Mephibosheth to join him at the royal table. Can you see it? Initially, Mephibosheth was too psychologically, physically, and spiritually damaged to believe or respond to the call. He had been down so long he could not even look up, which is the condition some men are in who have suffered in silence too long. I can imagine that during his lifetime, there was no one to attend to Mephibosheth's emotional needs, because everyone who lived there was in the same condition. **NOTE: It may be difficult for you to come out of where you are if you surround yourself with people who are suffering like you.** Mephibosheth may have even been too angry with God to reach out to Him just like many men in our contemporary society, and maybe even YOU!

You may be asking, "How could God allow me to go through what I have gone through?" Well the answer is simple.

God is God. Since you and I are here solely for His purpose, He can allow us to go through anything He chooses in order for His purpose and plan to be completed. Whether you know it or not, there is purpose in your suffering and the sooner you embrace the notion that God is in total control of your life, the more joy and peace you will experience. Mephibosheth accepted King David's royal invitation, which was the best decision he ever made.

God is inviting you to the King's table where all the fine china and linen are displayed for your pleasure. When you accept His invitation, you will enjoy the best food one could ever taste. The good news is you can stay in the palace all the days of your life. However, the first step is to accept the King's invitation. It will be the best decision you will ever make.

TAKE A FEW MOMENTS TO REFLECT ON HOW YOUR SECRET PAIN HAS AFFECTED YOU SPIRITUALLY!

PART IV

∞

STRATEGIES FOR OVERCOMING THE PAIN

Chapter 13

∞

A Multi-Systems Approach

Beloved I pray that you may prosper in all things and be in health, just as your soul prospers. 3 John 1:2

The participants of this project have done a wonderful job of sharing their insight and wisdom about manhood, and their personal struggles in fulfilling their roles as men. They have shared some of the things that cause them to cry and suffer from emotional pain. Now, they are going to discuss some of the positive strategies they personally use to promote good mental, physical, and spiritual health in order to do the great work that God is calling them to do.

A summary of the data revealed that the participants tend to cope with their pain by developing a closer relationship with God through prayer, devotional time, and fellowship with other Believers. These strategies are critical for all Christians to use for good emotional, physical, and spiritual health. They further reported that fishing, exercising, music, writing, sports, and work are helpful coping strategies. Just as all of these strategies can be very positive, some can also work in the reverse.

For example, men sometimes become overly involved in sports, exercise, and work activities in order to hide from their pain. As stated earlier in this book, it is very popular for men to immerse themselves in their work which can create problems in their relationships with spouses, children, and other important family members. These men maintain an ALL WORK AND NO PLAY philosophy. Further, men who are overworked tend to be more unhealthy and at-risk of developing serious physical and psychological diseases.

The participants of this project acknowledged the importance of connecting to the Spirit of God through an active prayer and devotional life in order to achieve true inner healing. Sadly, men who spend more time in the workplace, rarely have sufficient time for God and the things of God which is important for a healthy lifestyle.

I asked the participants to share their thoughts and beliefs about seeking professional help for mental health problems. They acknowledged that men will go to the medical doctor, even if they go kicking and screaming. However, they may be more reluctant to seek the help of a mental health professional. Therefore it was surprising that the majority of the participants of this project agreed that professional counseling is sometimes necessary and encouraged for themselves and other men in order to deal with some of the underlying issues they may face. Vernon summed it up like this:

I think counseling is a wonderful strategy for men. In fact, I have had counseling myself. My wife and I had marriage counseling. I think that if it had not been for the counselor, Lord knows where we would be today. We love each other, but those walls that you build up between love of self or self-ego can be too strong. I think that one of the problems men have in general is they feel that counseling is a negative word. It means something is wrong with me. When my wife first suggested counseling, the first question that came to my mind was: How am I going to go to counseling and have someone telling me about my problems? But I went and we needed that third person to help us through some really tough times. I think all men could probably use counseling because there are some things we need to get over.

A MULTI-SYSTEMS APPROACH TO HEALING

In my work, I have begun to see the value of promoting a Multi-Systems Approach to health and healing for both men and women because it really does take a variety of resources and strategies to help people to become healthy and whole. Multi-Systems approaches simply recognize the importance of community and family linkages and resources to assist people in achieving greater overall health and well-being.

In order for men to live a healthier lifestyle, I believe that God must be in the center of their lives. One must nurture one's relationship with God through prayer and fasting, praise and worship, devotional time, and through giving of one's time, talents, and treasury for the work of the Kingdom.

Next, the individual must be committed to participate in his own healing process. You can take the horse to the water but you cannot make him drink. Men who participate in their healing are really saying: **I ACKNOWLEDGE MY PAIN, I'M TIRED OF IT, AND I AM GOING TO DO SOMETHING ABOUT IT WITH GOD'S HELP.**

When men make the commitment to work on themselves, they become willing to conduct self-assessments in order to confront their issues. They are also willing to do the necessary work (i.e., going to the doctor without being forced or nagged by loving wives, family, and friends).

Men may not know how to take care of themselves because they have not been taught how to do so. Even though they may participate in outings and activities more than the women in their lives would like, they may not be taking care of themselves in a healthy way. Men sometimes may neglect themselves because they do not have good self-esteem and self-worth. Also, men who suffer from depression may hold a secret death wish, so they deliberately neglect themselves by failing to follow through with medical treatment.

Another reason men tend to neglect themselves is because they have been taught that their main function in the family is to take care of the needs of others, even at the risk of their own health and well-being. Those who constantly surrender their own needs and wants become bitter and resentful towards their spouses and children, and when they have reached their limit, they sometimes dump their venom out on their unsuspecting family members who have no clue as to how they are really feeling.

There is a great difference between acting selfishly and taking care of oneself. For example, a selfish man only cares about what he wants, how he wants it, and when he wants it. He doesn't usually care about the needs of others. It's His way or No Way!

But the man who exercises self-care is concerned about his needs as well as the needs of others. He is able to articulate and communicate those things he wants and needs, but is willing to negotiate so that everyone is happy in the end. I believe it is impossible to love others without loving God first, and then yourself. **YOU ARE WORTH IT!**

The next important system to consider is family. A healthy family system can be very important to one's overall health and well-being. Therefore, it is critical to nurture family relationships, especially with one's spouse and children. Men must begin to spend quality time with their wives and develop better strategies for communication. Marriage and family therapists can be very helpful in assisting couples to develop a better quality of marital bliss. As mentioned earlier in this book, many couples are lacking in a healthy blueprint for marriage, so it is important to seek help if necessary.

Similarly, men must become more active in the lives of their children. Failure to do so may cause both men and their children to suffer on the inside. There must be a concerted effort to communicate more effectively with the children in your home, and those not in your home to increase your participation in their lives. Sometimes, a third party is necessary to help you to achieve a healthier relationship with your children.

Another vital system to men's good health is the church. Church affiliation and membership can provide more than a good Sunday morning worship experience. The church can be an important resource for Spiritual development through weekly Bible studies and other relevant classes, and opportunities for prayer and fellowship with other men. Through these activities, men are given the opportunity to share with men who may have similar struggles, and to receive mentoring from more seasoned and spiritually mature men in the church. Men sometimes fail to get better because of the company they keep.

If you are married or single and hang out with men who lack Spiritual wisdom, that is not a good idea. One of two things is bound to happen: You will either be effective in influencing his life in a positive way, or he will be effective in influencing your life in a negative way. Marriages are threatened and sometimes destroyed because men and women spend quality time with folks who convince them that the grass looks greener on the other side. Well, it may look greener, but sometimes that grass may be more difficult to mow. Men need other male accountability partners for the purpose of prayer, support, encouragement, and when necessary, correction.

The final system of importance to men is the mental/medical health system. In order for men to overcome some of the inner pain and turmoil they are dealing with in secret, trained mental health and medical professionals can be helpful in the process. Some of you are carrying junk on the inside that just may kill you if you do not release it and let it go. Be sure to seek professionals who walk in harmony with God, so they will be better able to understand your Spiritual needs.

In addition, it is probably time for your annual physical, so please make the call to your primary physician today. You've wasted enough time, and time is of the essence. There are some steps you can take to begin your process of good health with the guidance of your doctor, such as developing a sensible diet, regular exercise, drinking 6-8 glasses of water daily, getting adequate rest and relaxation, and eliminating as much stress out of your life as possible. TAKE TIME OFF FOR VACATIONS AND GETAWAYS.

NOTE: Ladies you may have to help him in this area. Do not become angry when your husband does not plan vacations or getaways. Some men have not been taught how to do that, nor see the importance of taking off. Therefore, you may have to take the lead with joy. He will have a great time once you are away, and the two of you can get much needed rest and relaxation if you do not fight because he did not plan the trip.

Jesus said, *"I come that you might have life, and that you might have it more abundantly."* Failure to place God in the center of your life, failure to work on yourself and your family life, and failure to take advantage of the resources that are available to you, such as the church, and trained professionals, may prevent you from living the GOOD life God ordained for you to live.

Men you are very important to the women and children who love you, and the church and community you are called to serve. But more importantly, you are important to God. He knows and understands your pain, and He is willing and ready to dry your tear stained eyes. He is simply calling you to participate in the process. Whenever Jesus healed someone, He gave them clear instructions to participate in the process of their healing.

Are you ready to stop suffering on the inside in silence? God wants you to be healthy and whole, so now is your time to begin your new life. If you are ready to make the commitment to become psychologically, physically, and spiritually healthier, please consider completing the Commitment Form on the next page of this book, after spending quality time with God in prayer.

Initially, it may not be easy to make the necessary changes. But remember, you can do ALL things through Christ which strengthens you. Your success, however, will depend upon you developing a plan of success based on the Word of God. When you confront the possible barriers to your success, and develop strategies for overcoming them, you are in a better position to win.

The only way David was successful in slaying Goliath was his reliance on God and his preparation for the battle. He was equipped for the battle because he understood the enemy and used the right weapon. Some of you are losing the fight because you are using the wrong weapons. Ephesians 6:11 is encouraging you to "Put on the whole armor of God, that you may be able to stand against the wiles of the devil."

Once you have completed this process, your life will be so much better. Then you will be in the wonderful position of helping another man or boy to experience true inner healing and be set free. *"Therefore if the Son makes you free, you are free indeed."* John 8:36

COMMITMENT FORM

I, _____ hereby acknowledge that I have been crying internally and externally because of my emotional condition.

I hereby commit to participate in my healing by making the following steps:

1._____

2._____

3._____

I recognize that there are potential barriers that may hinder my progress in keeping my promises to God and me, such as:

1._____

2._____

3._____

However, I commit to utilize the following strategies presented in this book to help me to overcome these barriers:

1._____

2._____

3._____

Date: _____ Signature:_____

PART V

∞

EPILOGUE

Chapter 14

∞

A Message to Women

I would like to take this opportunity to thank every woman for allowing me to enter into the private world of your husbands, boyfriends, sons, brothers, fathers, grandfathers, and uncles. It is my prayer that you've been blessed by the insight of the 14 men who shared their experiences and wisdom to help us to gain a greater understanding about the emotional make-up of men we love and care about.

I encourage you to continue to demonstrate love and care for the men in your lives because God has equipped you with something special to be able to accomplish that goal. I realize that we are often asked to make the changes and adjustments in order to be in good relationships with men. That's probably true, because God made us and He knows we are capable of doing just that. Remember, we are designed to be the helper to our spouses, and probably all the men in our lives, and we were emotionally designed with that assignment in mind.

I would also like to invite you to study with intensity Proverbs 31 to gain more understanding about your role as a helper to your husband. In addition, ***The Elect Lady,*** by Bishop Eddie L. Long will help you to understand life's interruptions a little better, and the importance of knowing and accepting your assignment. When you are able to accept your assignment with joy, you will be better equipped to love your husband or the special man in your life, even when you do not want to.

I also encourage you to pray, pray, pray, and pray some more. The men in your life need your prayers. You must call their names out before the Lord everyday and ask God to strengthen, prosper, protect, and equip them. There is much power in prayer, and something happens when you intercede on behalf of someone else. It seems to move heaven.

Women ask me all the time what can they do to live in harmony with the men they love. So here goes!

WORK ON YOU!

Everyone has a past, filled with both good and bad experiences. Therefore, our thinking, feelings, and behaviors tend to be impacted in both positive and negative ways based on those past experiences. It is your job and mine, to embrace the positive experiences to reflect on God's goodness, kindness and unmerited favor towards us. Likewise, we should carefully consider the impact of those negative experiences on our lives and on the lives of the people around us. After evaluating your condition, you must seize the opportunity to make the necessary changes, modifications, and adjustments in your life so you can be healed of your past and live in harmony with others.

After working on you, you will be able to demonstrate forgiveness, respect, empathy, and praise for your husband or other important males in your life. Teach the children to honor and revere him, even if you do not believe he deserves it. Consider his feelings even if you do not believe he has any. Support him, even if his dreams seem far fetched. Allow him to be your hero, and most of all, allow him to lead.

I asked the men of this project to share some of the things they would like women to know. Two of the participants had this to say:

"I would like women to know that we are basically simple. We are not as complicated as we are made out to be. We are creatures of habit. We have this turtle shell, and underneath a heart and ego as fragile as an eggshell." Pastor Tommy

"For the mother who has a son without a father, help to create balance for him as best you can. Don't cheat him of your motherly love. He's going to need that, but give him the other things he needs so that he will be able to stand. You can't make him a man, but you can teach him what a good man should be. For women who are married to men, evaluate your relationship and find out what he needs, and see if you can give it to him. See if you can be part of the balanced solution or the balanced equation for his life, because there is a reason why you are together." Steven

Chapter 15

∞

A Message to Men

It has been my privilege and honor to write this book to provide some level of insight and understanding into the emotional world of my brothers. I am very grateful that I had a wonderful cadre of men to assist me in this project and I would like to thank them and you for allowing me, your sister, to take a stab at this very important topic.

There are many things I would like say to you in this last Chapter of the book. First, I want you to know how important you are to God first, your families, the churches you attend and serve, the communities you live and work in, and the entire world. Men have gotten such a bad reputation in society, and have had many negative experiences to make them doubt their importance. But I am here on behalf of all women to say, you are important to us and we need you. We need you to take care of yourselves mentally, physically, and spiritually so you can love us in a deeper more intimate way. Our sons need you and they are looking to you as the models we know you can be. Our daughters need you to be the example of the man they should be waiting for.

Second, I would like to encourage you to take advantage of the words of wisdom from the brothers who contributed to this project. While few in number, they were mighty in stature. I also hope you can benefit from some of my experiences in working with men in a professional setting. I have come to learn that too many of my brothers are crying on the inside. Therefore, consider speaking to a trained professional about your inner pain and secret suffering. I know it's difficult to talk about your personal pain, but you must in order to live a healthier and happier life.

Third, I would like to invite you to take time to increase your walk with God, because without Him we would all simply fail. You will need Him even more as you embark upon this journey of healing and wholeness. I realize that you may have experienced many disappointments in life, but God has never left you nor forsaken you, it just felt that way. He really wants to develop your faith and the more you trust Him, the more He will come through for you. Therefore, more prayer, more devotion, and more fellowship with other believers will certainly come in handy for the rest of your life.

As with the sisters, I would like to offer a few suggestions that may help you to have a healthier relationship with the women in your life.

WORK ON YOU!

I cannot emphasize enough the importance of one making the commitment to working on oneself. It is my prayer that you will complete the Commitment Form so that you can hold yourself accountable to continue to improve in your mental, physical, and spiritual health.

Take time to learn more about your wife's needs. She will teach you if you allow her to. Stop withholding the love from her when you don't have the words to communicate your true feelings. Forgive her, support her, respect her, and pray for her. Allow her to enter into your world, and give her the opportunity to help you. She was designed for that purpose and that is why she is so insistent on doing so. Lastly, spend quality time with your wife and children. They are doing everything possible to get your attention. Remember, the true sign of a great man is not how much money he has, or the great accomplishments and/or contributions he has made in the world to help others. Rather, it is how he is viewed by his wife and children.

The men of this project have written some parting words of wisdom just with you in mind. We will close this page of our journey with a few of those messages of encouragement:

"I think it would be great if men could bond more together, in our churches, society, or men's group to have inner discussions about some of the things that we discussed during the course of this

project. We need to get things off our chest with another man and to accept ideas from men with no male egos. Just let yourself be free and relaxed. There is someone out there that you can share and talk with." Vernon

"It's alright to be vulnerable and to express your feelings. It doesn't make you any less of a man. In fact, it makes you more of a man because when you express how you feel you are able to show your true feelings. That means you are not running away from your feelings. A real man stands up to whatever it is that is coming against him. So if you are having some feelings in your heart that need to come out, be a man, and let it come out. Don't worry what others will think. If another man says you are not a man because you are expressing yourself, then he is not really a man." Philip

"Ask God to give you the strength to endure, because it is too hard for you alone. But the Word teaches, 'I can do all things through Christ which strengthens me'. Put all your trust in Him because He will never let you down." Rev. Phillips

SELECTED BIBLIOGRAPHY

Harrell, S. P. (2000). A multidimensional conceptualization of racism-related stress. Implications for the well-being of people of color. American Journal of Orthopsychiatry, 70, 42-57.

Jakes, T.D. (2004). He-Motions: Even strong men struggle. New York: G.P. Putnum's Sons.

Long, E.L. (2008). The elect lady. Kensington, PA: Whitaker House.

Morrow, G. (2008). Create your blueprint for good success. Upland, CA: Shining Glory Publications, Inc.

Morrow, G. (2006). Keeping it Real! 7 steps toward a healthier you. Upland, CA: Shining Glory Publications, Inc.

Morrow, G. (2005). Strengthening the ties that bind: A guide to a healthy marriage. Upland, CA: Shining Glory Publications, Inc.

Morrow, G. (2003). Too broken to be fixed? A spiritual guide to inner healing. Upland, CA: Shining Glory Publications, Inc.

SELECTED BIBLIOGRAPHY

Phillips, H. E., & Phillips, H. (2003). Leaving a legacy of hope: A guide to a successful marriage. Upland, CA; Shining Glory Publications, Inc.

Staff of the Washington Post (2007). Being a black man at the corner of progress and peril. New York: Washington Post Public Affairs.

White, J.L. & Cone, III, J.H. (1999). Black man emerging: Facing the past and seizing the future. New York: W.H. Freeman & Co.

Resources

Hotline

National Domestic Violence Hotline – (800) 799-7233
National Suicide Hotline – (800) SUICIDE
Rape, Abuse, Incest National Network (800) 656-HOPE

Internet

www.gloriamorrow.com
www.gap-ministries.com
www.blackhealth.com
www.cabwhp.org
www.hopeallianz.com
www.abpsi.org
(Association of Black Psychologists)

Additional Books

Saving our Last Nerve – Marilyn Martin
Black Pain – Terrie Williams

Resources

Additional Books & DVD's by Dr. Gloria Morrow

- *Too Broken to be Fixed? A Spiritual Guide to Inner Healing*
- *Suffer in Silence No More*
- *Strengthening the Ties that Bind: A Guide to a Healthy Marriage*
- *Keeping it Real! 7 Steps Toward a Healthier You*
- *Create Your Blueprint for Good Success*
- *A Life Plan Portfolio (LPP)*